CW01360159

© Macmillan Publishers Limited, 1984
All rights reserved. No part of this publication may be reproduced or transmitted, in any form or by any means, without permission.

Printed in Hong Kong

ISBN 0 333 37305 7

First published in 1984 by
Macmillan Children's Books
a division of Macmillan Publishers Limited,
4 Little Essex Street, London WC2R 3LF
and Basingstoke

Associated companies in
New York, Toronto, Dublin,
Melbourne, Johannesburg and Delhi

Designer
Julian Holland

Picture researcher
Stella Martin

Artists
Fred Anderson
Sara Pooley

Editors
Penny Farrant
Miranda Smith

Photocredits:
All-Sport Photographic Ltd
Ajax News & Feature Service
Austin Rover Group
Biofotos
Peter J Bish
Boeing
BP Oil Ltd
British Aerospace
British Engineerium
British Hovercraft Corporation
British Petroleum
J Allan Cash Ltd
Bruce Coleman Ltd
Custom Car
Findus Ltd
Ford Aerospace
L Gardner & Sons Ltd
The Goodyear Tire & Rubber Company
Hawker Siddeley Group
Michael Holford
Eric and Michael Hoskins
Alan Hutchison Library
Mat Irvine
Krauss Maffei
Lake & Elliot
National Maritime Institute Ltd
Natonal Motor Museum
Natural History Photographic Agency
Overseas Containers Ltd
Picturepoint Ltd
Premaphotos Wildlife
R C Riley
Rolls-Royce Ltd
Rolls-Royce Motors
Ann Ronan Picture Library
Royal Astronomical Society
Ruston Gas Turbines Ltd
Mark Shearman
Shell
Nigel Snowdon
Westland Helicopters Ltd
ZEFA

The Science of
Movement

Ralph Hancock

M
MACMILLAN

Contents

Newton's laws of motion — 4
Movement in plants — 7
Muscles and how animals move — 10
Movement in simple machines — 16
Friction — 19
Wheels and tracks — 22
Piston engines — 25
Steam engines — 28
Turbines and fans — 31
Electric motors — 34
Conveyors, pipelines, cableways — 37
Ships and boats — 40
Sails, propellors, wings, rotors — 43
How animals and helicopters fly — 46
Aircraft and gliders — 49
Bird shapes and movements — 52
Other flying creatures — 55
Shapes and controls of aircraft — 58
Orbit and satellites — 61
Index — 65

◁ Men's 400 metres relay race.

Newton's laws of motion

All movement, of everything from a galaxy of stars to a speck of dust, obeys three very simple natural laws. These laws are called Newton's laws of motion, after the great scientist Sir Isaac Newton who discovered them.

Newton's first law of motion says that any moving object goes on moving in a straight line and at a steady speed unless an outside force acts on it. If it changes direction or speed then a force has made it do so.

The second law of motion says that when a force acts on an object, the rate at which the object's speed changes depends on the strength of the force. Think what happens when you ride a bicycle. The more effort you put into turning the pedals, the faster you go. Here your effort is the force, and the rate at which the speed of the bicycle changes depends on the strength of your effort.

The third law of motion says that for every action there is an equal and opposite reaction. If you wear a pair of roller skates and throw something heavy in front of you, you will find you roll backwards. In doing so you are obeying the third law. You are being forced backwards with exactly the same force that you used to throw the thing in the opposite direction.

Newton's laws may not seem obvious

You know that if you give a ball on flat ground a push it will stop quite soon all by itself. But the first law of motion says that this can only happen if an outside force acts on the ball. So where is the force? In this case it is friction, an invisible force which slows all moving things down. Gravity is another invisible force which might make you think the first law is wrong. It will change the direction of a moving object that has been thrown up in the air by pulling it back to earth. Neither friction nor gravity affect the truth of Newton's laws.

The first law
Any moving object goes on moving in a straight line and at a steady speed until an outside force acts on it. If it is not moving, it stays still until a force acts on it. You have to give a car a hard push to start it moving. Once it is moving, the force of friction will eventually bring it to rest again. You too can slow it down. Here your pull is the force acting on the car to change its speed.

The second law

Austin Metro 1.0 HLE

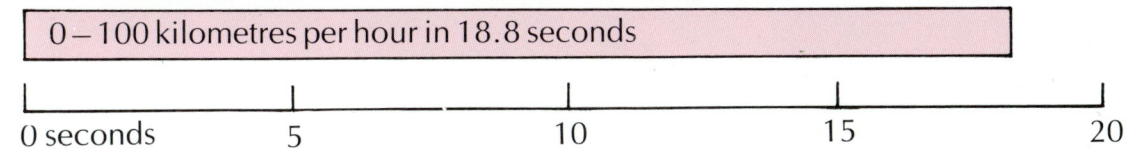

| 0 – 100 kilometres per hour in 18.8 seconds |

0 seconds 5 10 15 20

When a force acts on an object, the rate at which the object's speed changes depends on the strength of the force. The car above is an ordinary model but the one below has been 'hotted up'. It has about twice the power of the ordinary model and so can reach the same speed nearly twice as quickly.

MG Metro Turbo

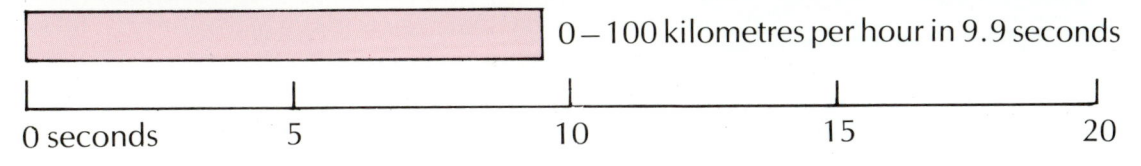

| 0 – 100 kilometres per hour in 9.9 seconds |

0 seconds 5 10 15 20

The third law

For every action there is an equal and opposite reaction. When you fire a gun the force of the explosion sends the bullet speeding forward. It also throws the gun, and the person holding it, backward with exactly the same force. The bullet travels forward further and faster than the gun moves backward because it is so much lighter. But the force acting on it is the same, just working in the opposite direction.

Sir Isaac Newton 1642–1727

Newton was born in a small house in the village of Woolsthorpe in Lincolnshire. His mother was a widow and the family did not have a great deal of money. The local schools were good but even so Isaac was a bad pupil. He spent most of his time making models and doing experiments. Despite this, he managed to get into Cambridge University where he was fascinated by mathematics. In 1665, when plague swept through England, Newton fled home for two years.

One day, as he was sitting in the orchard thinking about his theories, he saw an apple fall from a tree. Wondering why things fell like this, Newton worked out an explanation based on the force we call gravity. He developed this further to produce the laws of gravity and then the laws of motion.

Newton made many other discoveries in his lifetime. He did a lot of work on mathematics and on light and colour. He also invented the reflecting telescope, a kind which is still used in big astronomical telescopes. Magic and alchemy – the turning of metal into gold – were other great interests of his. In those days they were thought quite respectable sciences.

Movement in plants

Plants move in all sorts of ways and for different reasons. Although there are a few water plants which drift around quite freely on the current, most plants are fixed to the spot by their roots. They move as they grow or spread their seeds and certain types even move to get the food they need.

The speed at which plants grow varies tremendously. Some types of bamboo grow as much as 30 centimetres a day, almost fast enough to see them moving. Others, like certain lichens found in polar regions, grow so slowly that they may live for thousands of years.

Plants need light to provide the energy they need to make food in their leaves. Many move their leaves in order to get as much as possible. This is why houseplants near a window tend to turn their leaves towards the light that comes from outside. Maranta, a common houseplant, opens its leaves by day to take in sunlight and then closes them again at night.

Plants spread themselves or their seeds in all sorts of ways. Certain types spread by sending out suckers underground from which new plants grow up. All the elms that used to grow in England are thought have spread from one tree in this way.

▽ This is a sundew, a type of plant which eats insects. Here it is trapping a damselfly. The leaves of the plant have spiky hairs on them which are shiny and sticky. These attract insects. When the plant feels a touch the hairs bend over to trap the insect. The plant then produces a juice which digests the victim. Few insects react fast enough to escape from the plant.

◁ These houseplants are bending towards the window in order to get as much light as they can on their leaves. They lean this way because the shaded side of their stems grows faster.

▽ This tiny bracken shoot is soft and young but it has forced its way through a layer of tarmac. Growing plants push up with enormous strength. Some have even been known to crack concrete slabs or make buildings collapse.

Other plants reproduce from seeds and these are moved around in many different ways. The seeds of ash trees have wings so that when they get picked up by the wind they are carried quite a distance. Dandelion seeds are spread in the same way but they have parachutes to help them drift in the air instead of wings. Conkers, the seeds of horse chestnut trees, are also well designed to move. Because they are so smooth and round they roll a long way when their spiky cases fall from the tree and split open. Other plants have seed pods which explode when ripe. Broom is like this and the explosion is strong enough to throw its seeds several metres away from the plant.

Animals move seeds

Animals are responsible for moving many types of seed even though they may not realize this. Sometimes the seeds cling to their coats so that they get carried around as the animal moves. This often happens with burdock seeds which have little hooks on them. In other cases animals eat fruit and the seed of the fruit is then spread around when it passes through undigested. Acorns and other large tree seeds are often moved by squirrels as they build up their winter stores. If the conditions are right, a new plant will grow wherever seed is dropped. Some seeds can wait for years or even centuries to start growing.

Sensitive plants
▷ This is a leaf of a kind of mimosa called a 'sensitive plant' or a 'touch-me-not'. Whenever anything touches it, the leaf folds up within a second. This has happened in the photograph below. The plant reacts in this way in order to protect itself. Here the danger comes from an animal which might eat it. After a few minutes of being curled up the leaf reopens.

▷ The leaf of a sensitive plant has special cells just at the point where the tiny leaflets are attached to the centre stem. This point acts as a hinge. When the cells are touched, they suddenly lose moisture and collapse so that the hinge closes. If the plant is touched strongly enough all the leaves may wilt in this way so that the plant collapses completely.

Muscles and how animals move

All animals, from the tiniest insects to the largest whales, use muscles to move. Most muscles are fixed to the skeleton at either end. They work by shortening so that they pull the two parts of the skeleton together. Muscles can only pull, they cannot push, so each joint has to have a muscle on either side, one to move it each way. Even animals without skeletons use pairs of muscles to bend back and forth.

There are two kinds of muscle. Those which we can move when we want to are called voluntary muscles. Those that do their job automatically without us having to think about them are called involuntary muscles. They work many organs in our bodies like our heart and lungs. Both kinds of muscles are made to move by nerves. These work like wires sending electric signals round to all our different parts. Moving a muscle, however small, uses up energy, which comes from the food we eat.

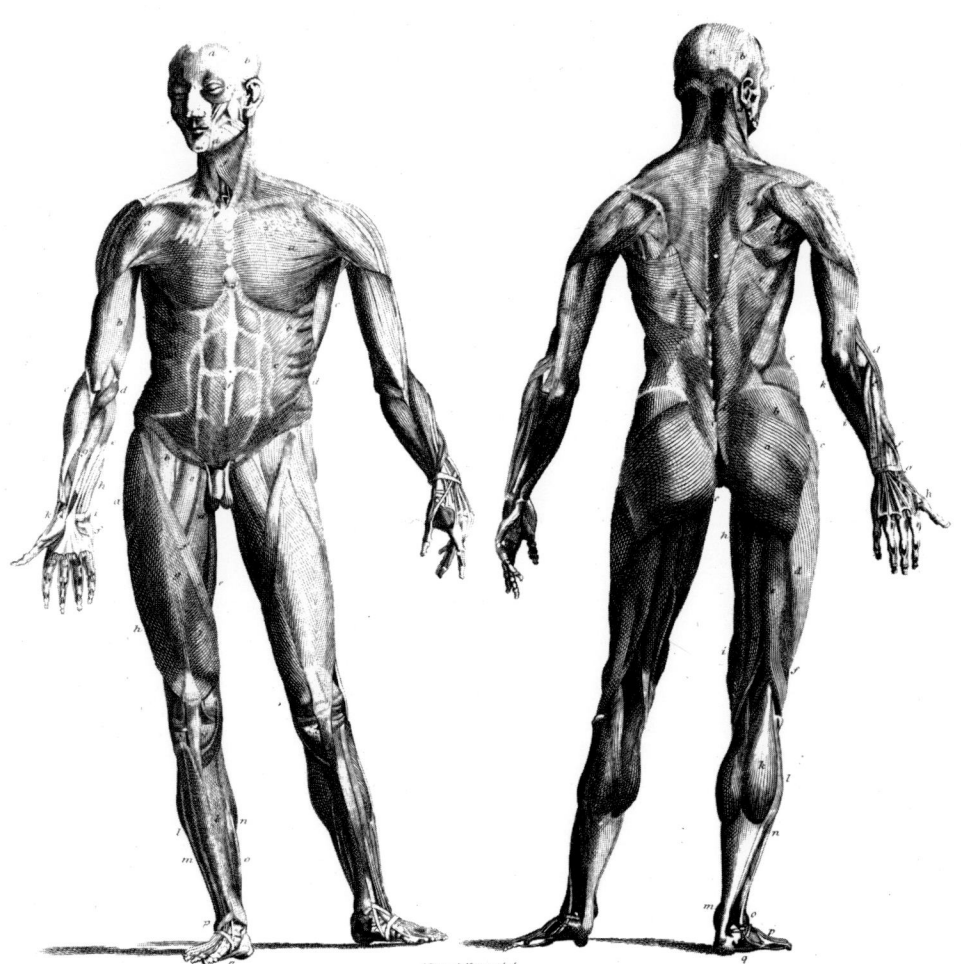

△ Here you can see the outer layer of muscles on the human body. All of them are voluntary muscles but even so only a few of the large ones like this are shown. There are others under this layer, as well as countless smaller involuntary muscles.

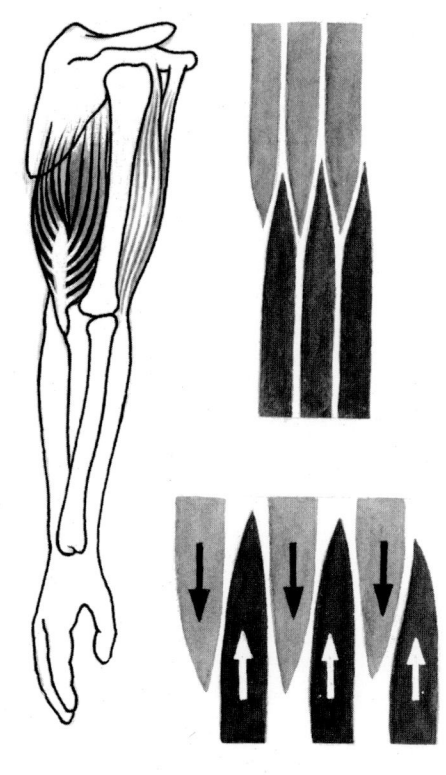

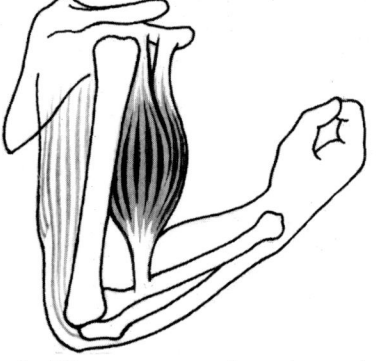

△ The top two drawings show the biceps muscle in the upper arm, which pulls up the lower arm. When it pulls it gets thicker. The lower drawings show why. They show the tiny strands inside each fibre of muscle. When a nerve tells the strands to shorten, they slide together and overlap. This causes the bundle of strands to widen out. It is what happens when you flex your muscles.

△ The African cheetah is a hugely powerful animal with well developed muscles. It can reach speeds of 96 kilometres per hour when chasing its prey. But it runs out of energy fairly quickly so it cannot keep going like this for long.

◁ Impalas cannot move as fast as cheetahs but they are more efficient runners. They cover huge distances at a steady gallop. Providing they escape the cheetah's first attack they can probably outrun it to safety.

Animals that move on legs use them in various ways. Those with four legs move them in different ways as they go from a walk to a trot and then to a gallop. The exact pattern they make depends on the type of animal it is. Compare the impala and cheetah on page 11 and see the different movements they use.

Kangaroos hardly use their front legs at all. They hop with both their hind legs together and use their tails for balance. Centipedes, which have hundreds of tiny hair-like legs, move them in waves. As they crawl it looks as though ripples are sweeping down the lines of legs. Other animals which move in strange ways include monkeys who swing from branch to branch using their arms and tails, and crabs which walk sideways.

▷ Snakes get about perfectly well without any legs at all. They move by wriggling their bodies to and fro in S-shaped patterns. This makes them go slightly sideways rather than straight ahead. You can see this very clearly from the marks left by the American sidewinder snake on the right. It moves sideways like this in order to cross over the loose desert sand.

◁ Animals that walk on two legs, like people and ostriches, have to be able to balance. Watch someone as they walk or notice how you do it yourself. As you put each foot forward you shift your whole body to that side so that your weight is over that foot. When you walk you always have one foot on the ground. When running both feet are in the air together at times.

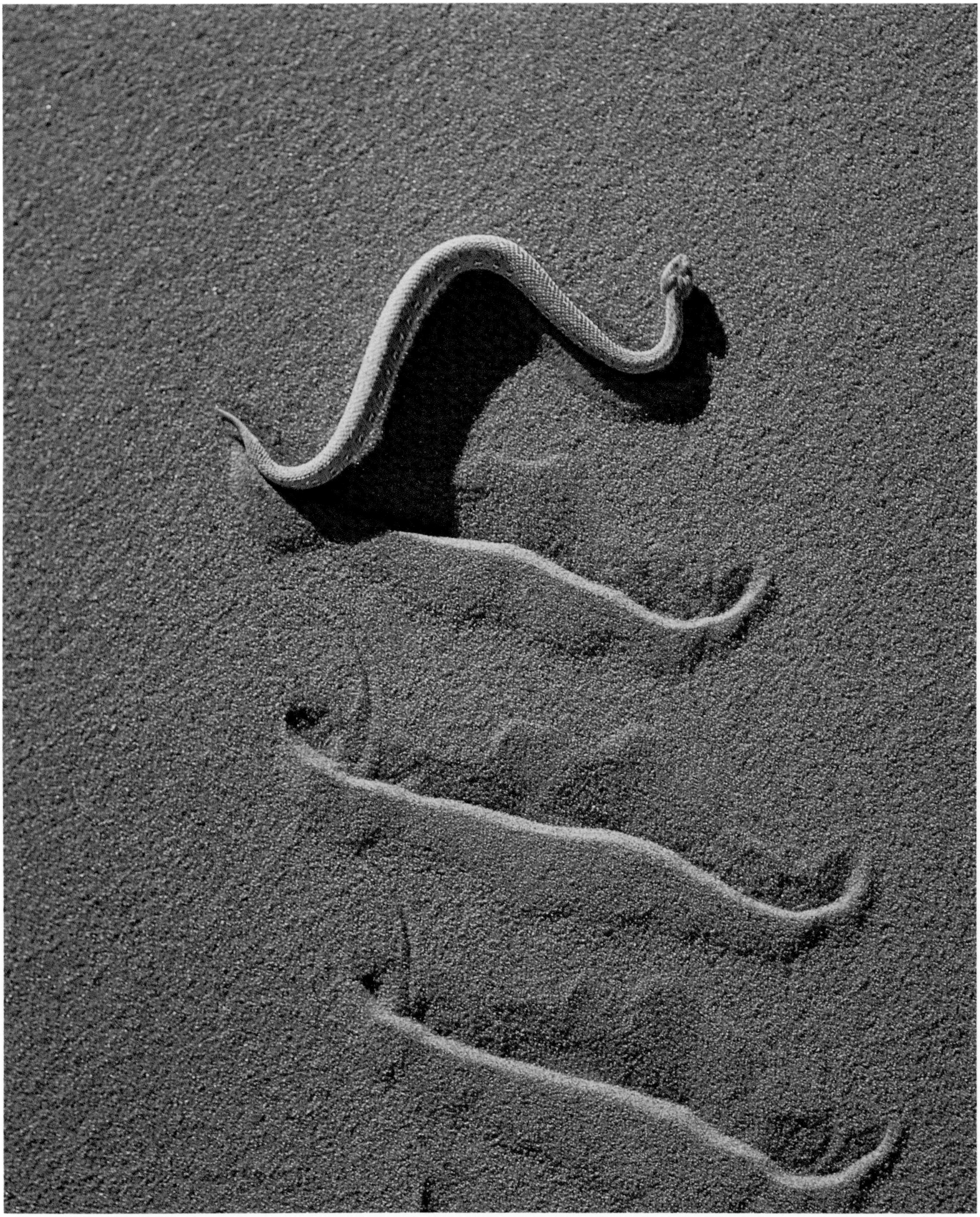

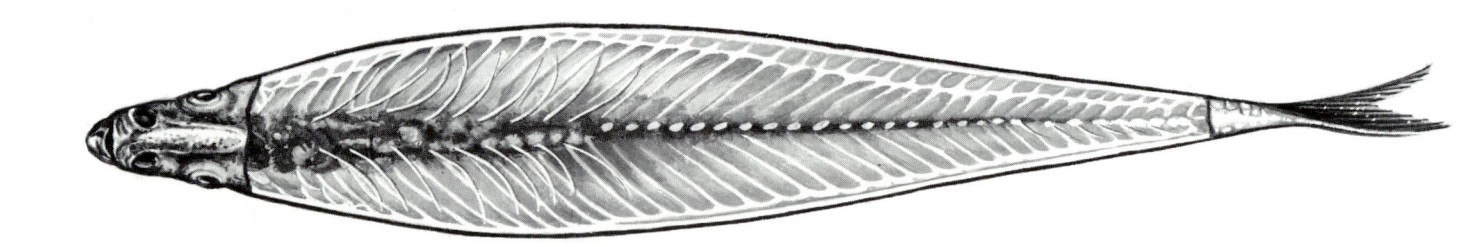

How fish move

◁ Fish swim by curving their bodies and tails backwards and forwards in S shapes. Their fins are used for steering. As you can see above, their swimming muscles are arranged in neat rows fixed to the backbone down the centre. The most efficient swimmers are smooth, streamlined fish such as herring. These fancy goldfish move fairly slowly because their odd shapes do not slip through the water smoothly.

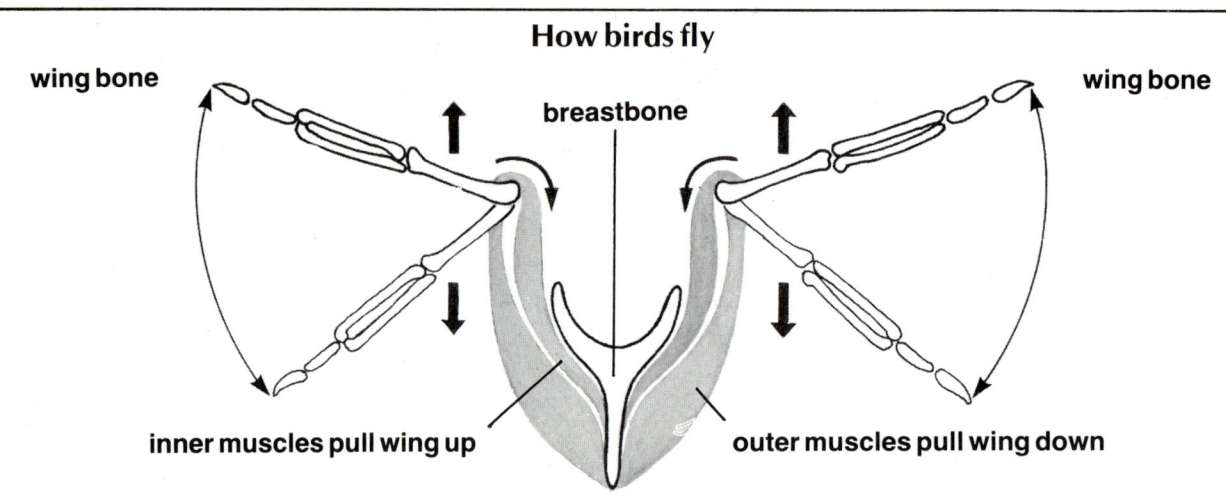

How birds fly

wing bone — **breastbone** — **wing bone**

inner muscles pull wing up — **outer muscles pull wing down**

Birds need large, powerful muscles to fly. Their flight muscles are fixed to the wing bones at the top and the breastbone at the bottom. When the inner set of muscles shorten they pull the wings up. The outer set of muscles, which are larger, then pull the wings down. Both sets are firmly anchored to the bird in a deep keel on its breastbone. Together they make up as much as a quarter of the bird's total weight.

All the animals mentioned so far have skeletons with muscles surrounding their bones. Insects are not like this. They have a skeleton on the outside with muscles inside it. Their outer skeleton or casing is like a jointed tube made of tough, springy material.

Their legs and wings are fixed to sections of tube at the front of the body called the thorax. The wings are very thin and flat and are stiffened by a network of veins. The legs are hollow with muscles inside. The back part of the body, the abdomen, is made of several tube sections joined together. It plays little part in the insect's movement.

The three drawings running across the bottom of the page show how you would find the insect's muscles arranged if you cut across its middle. They work in pairs. One set pulls the wings up and the other pulls them down. Both sets of muscles are completely inside the thorax.

Although most insects have two pairs of wings, they generally move both pairs together. But there are many types which have other arrangements. Flies, dragonflies and beetles are like this. Some of them are shown and described on pages 55-57. Other insects such as grasshoppers or earwigs hardly ever fly. Many insects do not even have wings.

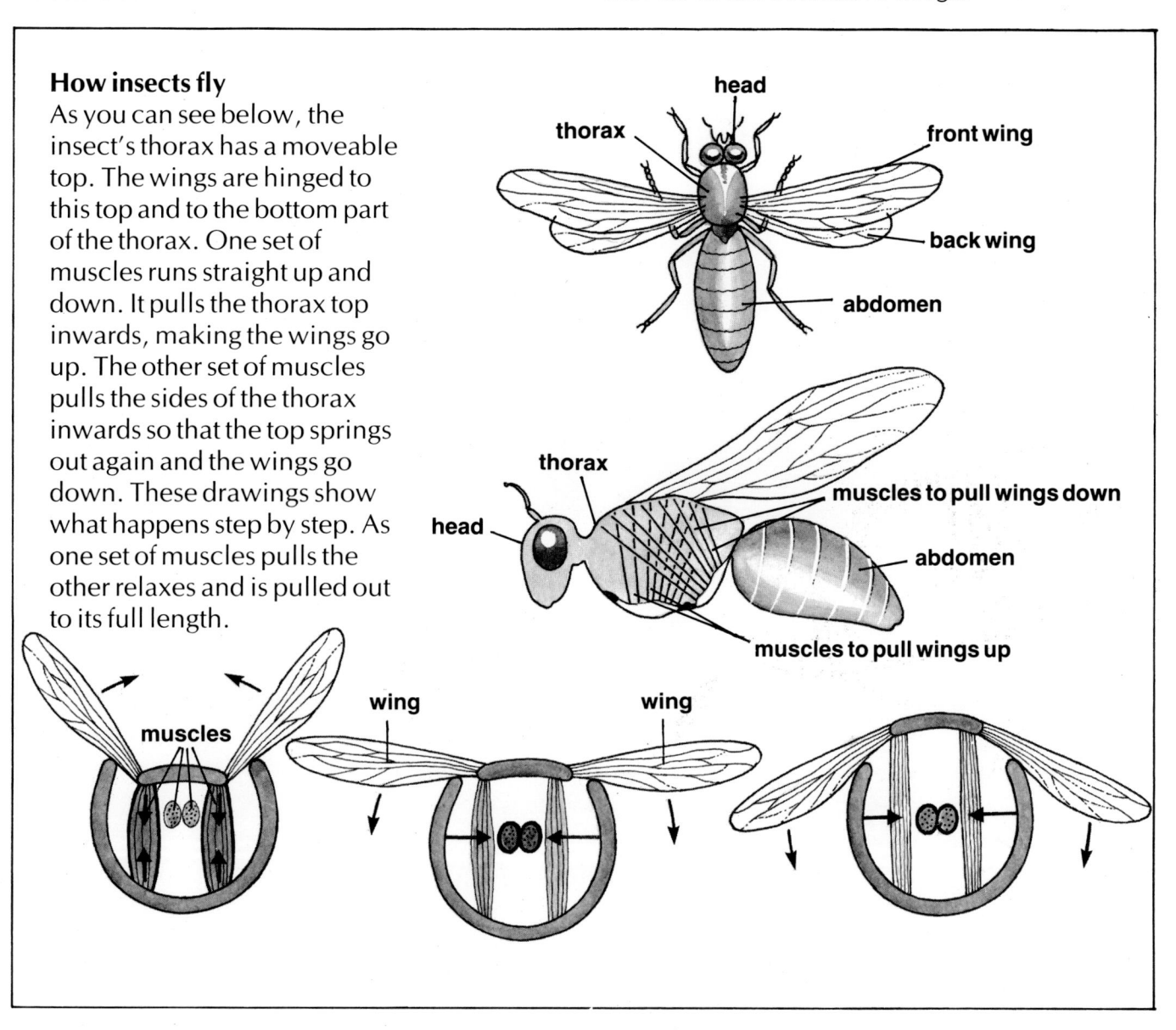

How insects fly

As you can see below, the insect's thorax has a moveable top. The wings are hinged to this top and to the bottom part of the thorax. One set of muscles runs straight up and down. It pulls the thorax top inwards, making the wings go up. The other set of muscles pulls the sides of the thorax inwards so that the top springs out again and the wings go down. These drawings show what happens step by step. As one set of muscles pulls the other relaxes and is pulled out to its full length.

Movement in simple machines

Machines do not have to be complicated and even the simplest can help us move things. All those on the next three pages are useful because they 'trade' effort for something else.

Suppose there is an object too heavy for you to lift with your bare hands. It weighs 100 kilograms and has to be raised one metre. An engineer might say that the effort required to do this is 1000 newton metres – a newton is a force equal to one-tenth of a kilogram. Using a lever would be one way in which you could move it. The lever can be arranged under the heavy object so that when you push its free end down two metres the object will be lifted by one metre. You have to push the lever with a force of 500 newtons for this to happen. By applying 500 newtons over a distance of two metres you are using an effort of 1000 (that is, 500 x 2) newton metres. You have applied a force of only half the object's weight but you have done so over twice the distance it has moved. All the lever has done is 'trade' strength for distance.

Levers
Levers can be used to help open heavy lock gates like these. The lever is fixed to the top of the gate. The distance from its end to the hinge of the gate is four times the distance from the hinge to the centre of the gate. This means that a 500 newtons push on the lever will provide the 2000 newtons force needed to open the gate. But the man pushing the lever has to walk four times as far as the gate moves for this to happen.

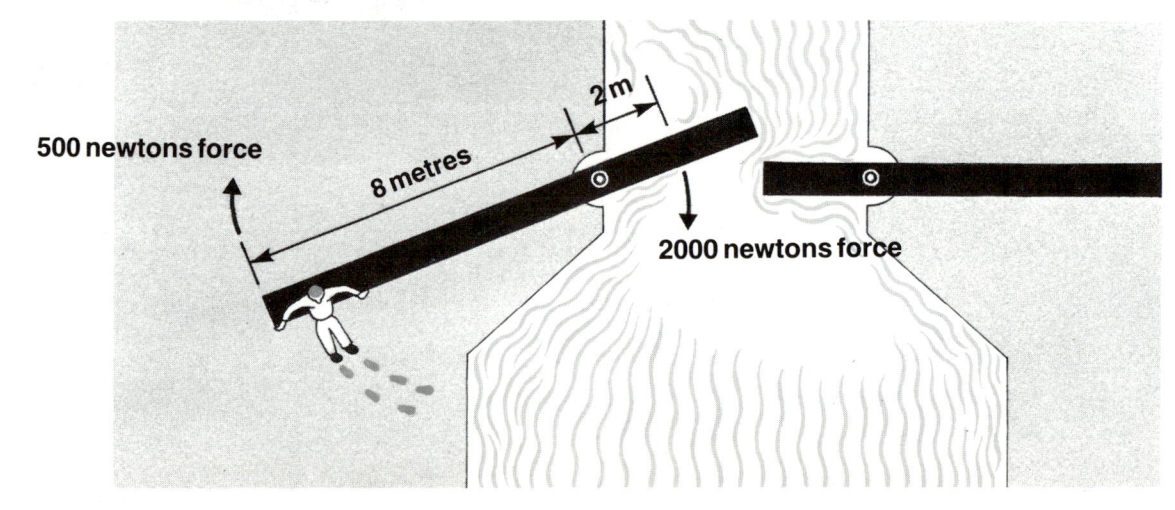

Pulleys

Pulleys are used to haul heavy ship's rigging. The single pulley below is arranged so that if the man pulls the rope four metres with 500 newtons force, the pulley hauls the sail two metres with 1000 newtons force. Often several pulleys are used together to give an increase of four or eight times the force applied. Some hoists used to lift engines out of cars are arranged in this way. Single pulleys are often used to lift washing lines.

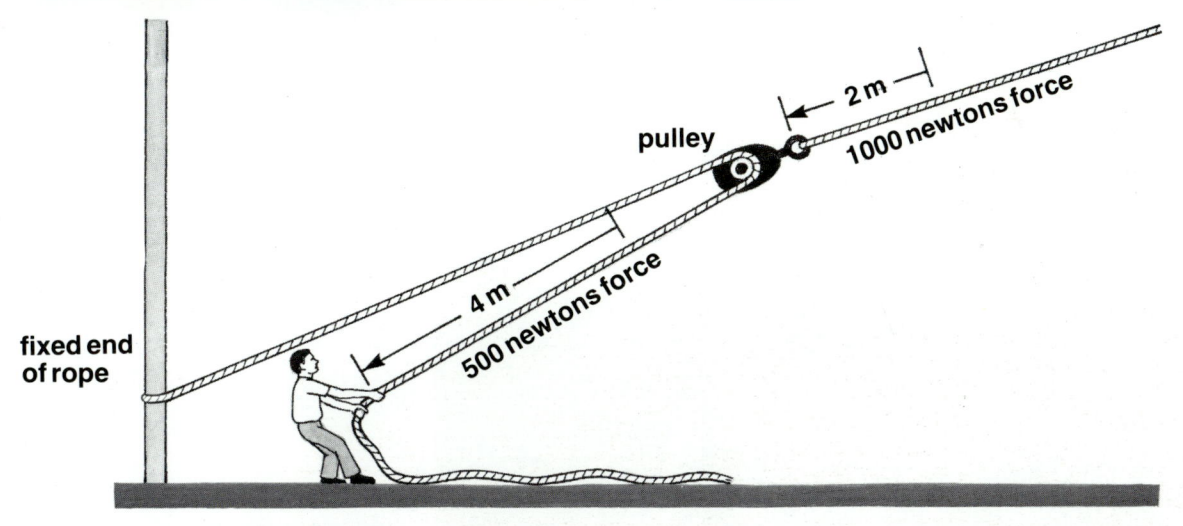

Levers and pulleys are only two examples of simple machines. Another is the screw, used in presses and car jacks. The screw has a handle. You have to turn the handle a long way in order to get the screw to move a little way. Sometimes the screw moves as little as one-hundreth of the distance that the handle is turned. This means that it exerts a force 100 times as large as that applied to the handle.

Gears are another type of simple machine. They use wheels which interlock with each other. A small gear wheel with ten teeth can be fitted together or 'meshed' with a larger wheel with 30 teeth. The smaller wheel will then have to turn three times in order to make the big wheel go round once.

This arrangement means that the large wheel turns with three times the turning force or 'torque'. This is what happens when you use a low gear to go up a hill on a bicycle. Large and small gears can be used the other way round to increase speed but then they reduce torque.

Water wheels

This water wheel lifts water from a stream to a higher channel. The flow of the stream turns it. Water is caught in buckets attached to the rim. These are then carried to the top and tipped out. It takes a lot of water flowing under the wheel to raise a little water to the higher channel.

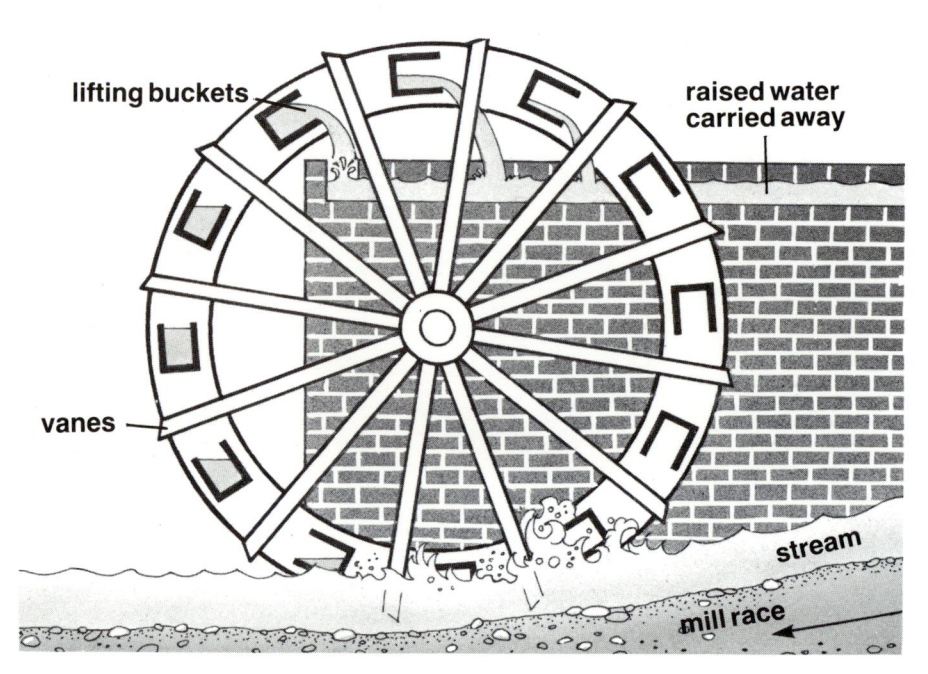

lifting buckets

raised water carried away

vanes

stream

mill race

Hydraulic jacks

◁ Jacks like this one are used in garages to raise cars. It is a hydraulic jack, which means that it uses a liquid (usually oil) to transfer pressure. The handle is moved a long way to lift the car a short distance. To lift a car, the handle is pumped up and down. The jack is let down by opening a tap which lets the oil out of the large cylinder.

Friction

Moving anything uses up energy because things never slide completely smoothly. The energy is said to be lost in 'friction'. Friction occurs whenever two surfaces rub together. It is a form of resistance which affects every moving thing on Earth.

When a car moves steadily along a level road, all the mechanical energy is lost in friction. There is friction between all the moving parts in the engine, friction in the transmission and friction between the car wheels and the road. There is also friction between the car and the air it moves through as it goes forwards. This happens because when air is pushed aside and forced to flow over a car's surface, it resists the car's movement.

Friction produces heat

Friction even happens in machines in which highly polished bearings have been specially used to help the different parts move together as smoothly as possible. The energy which goes into friction is given off as heat. This is why machines feel hot after they have been running for some time.

It is only in space, where there is no air, that an object can move without friction. This means that once it has been given a push to start moving, it will go on for ever. On Earth friction slows and eventually stops everything.

△ Drag racing tests how quickly cars gain speed from a standing start. The cars that take part are specially built for this and are called dragsters. Their very powerful engines tend to make the car tyres spin and lose their grip. That is why such enormous tyres are used. The bigger the tyre, the better it grips the ground. This improves the car's hold on the road. The friction creates a great deal of heat which burns the tyres so that they give off the clouds of blue smoke you can see here.

△ Jet aircraft are streamlined to reduce their air resistance. But when they slow down to land they use friction. The plane's air brakes are the door-like flaps sticking out by its tail. When they are extended, the amount of air resistance is increased so the plane slows down.

◁ Boats and ships are slowed down by resistance from the water. Hovercraft avoid this by riding on a 'cushion' of air blown downwards by huge fans.

In order to cut down the amount of energy lost in friction, moving surfaces are often lubricated. This means that they are coated by a thin layer of lubricant which helps them to move more smoothly. The lubricant may be a solid, liquid or gas but the one used to lubricate most common machines is oil.

Some forms of friction are very important to us. The friction between your feet and the ground allows you to keep standing. If it did not exist, your feet would just slide as soon as you tried to move. Cars could not work without it either. If there were no friction, the wheels would spin uselessly. Brakes also rely on friction. All the energy from the moving part turns into heat and sound when brakes are applied.

▷ The movements of this skater are lubricated by water. His weight makes the ice below the skate blade melt as he passes over it. So the skater slides on a layer of water, which reduces friction in the same way as oil does in a machine. The cold of the surrounding ice freezes the water again as soon the skater has passed.

△ Airliners need very powerful brakes to stop them as they land. The brake discs are between the wheels. Pads of tough material are pressed onto both sides of them to bring the plane to a halt.

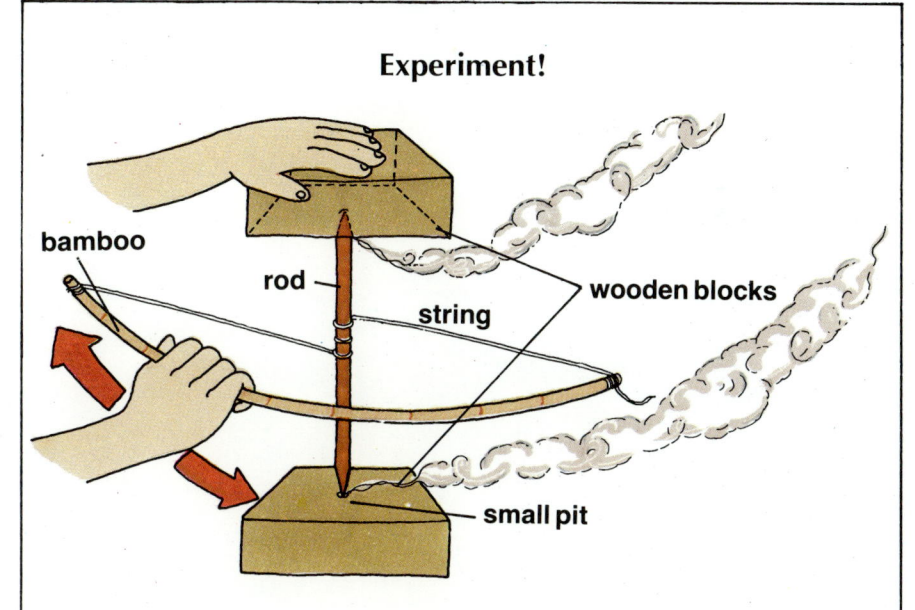

Experiment!

Fire drills are used in many parts of the world to light fires. In order to make one yourself you need a round wooden rod, two very dry wood blocks, a length of thin bamboo and some thin string. Sharpen both ends of the rod and then fix it into small pits in the centre of each block. Make the bamboo and string into a bow like the one shown above. You will have to move the bow from side to side on the rod for quite some time in order to produce enough heat from the friction to make a fire. Feed the flame with little pieces of paper.

Wheels and tracks

Wheels are something only a machine can have – plants and animals cannot. This is because a wheel turns, so it has to be separate from the machine it is part of. The limbs of animals and leaves of plants would not survive if they were cut off from their bodies or stems in this way. They need to be linked the whole time to supplies of blood or other vital fluids. If they were to turn like a wheel the tubes carrying these supplies would get twisted and the animal or plant would die. Wheels have to be able to turn freely to work properly.

△ A man on a bicycle is easily the most efficient animal on land. He can go hundreds of kilometres non-stop at a steady speed of 25 kilometres an hour. When cycling he uses only 40% of the energy it would take him to walk that far.

◁ Tracked vehicles can be enormous. This one was used to move the Saturn moon rockets to their launch pad. It took hours to cover the five kilometres because it crawled along so slowly. The cars on the road beside it give an idea of its vast size.

△ Earth-moving vehicles have huge tyres, each of which costs about as much as a large car. They measure over two metres in diameter.

◁ This car is a specially built lightweight one, designed to take part in a fuel economy race. Each vehicle in the race is given a litre of fuel. The one that travels the greatest distance is the winner.

Wheels reduce friction and so make it easier to move things. A heavy load that is impossible to carry or drag can be put on wheels. Then a light push will move it. In this way wheels both save energy and shift things too heavy to lift. They are used everywhere – on cars and trains and as castors on all sorts of furniture, heavy equipment and machines.

In order to make wheels even more efficient, ball bearings are sometimes fitted between the wheel and its axle. This reduces the amount of friction and makes the wheel turn smoothly.

Tracks are often used instead of wheels when heavy loads have to be moved over soft ground. They are like a set of wheels carrying its own metal road with it. The tracks work better than wheels alone because they spread the load's weight over a larger area.

◁ The Indian bullock cart is one of the simplest wheeled vehicles but it does a good job. Its sturdy spoked wheels look as if they are about to fall off. In fact they have to be fitted loosely like this so that they can move sideways to follow the ruts in the road. If they were firmly fixed they would break. When an 'improved' cart with rubber-tyred wheels and a metal axle was tried, it was a failure.

Experiment!

Try this competition with your friends. The idea is to see who can make the strongest wheel. Everyone needs four sheets of stiff paper about the same size as a page in this book, and some glue. They have to use these to make one wheel with a diameter of 20 centimetres. A pencil should be used for the wheel's axle. To judge whose wheel is best make a wheelbarrow like the one shown here. The winner's wheel is the one which carries the heaviest load without collapsing.

Before you build your wheel think carefully about its design. The rim and hub and parts between must be as stiff as you can make them. But you can only use the four sheets of paper you have been given.

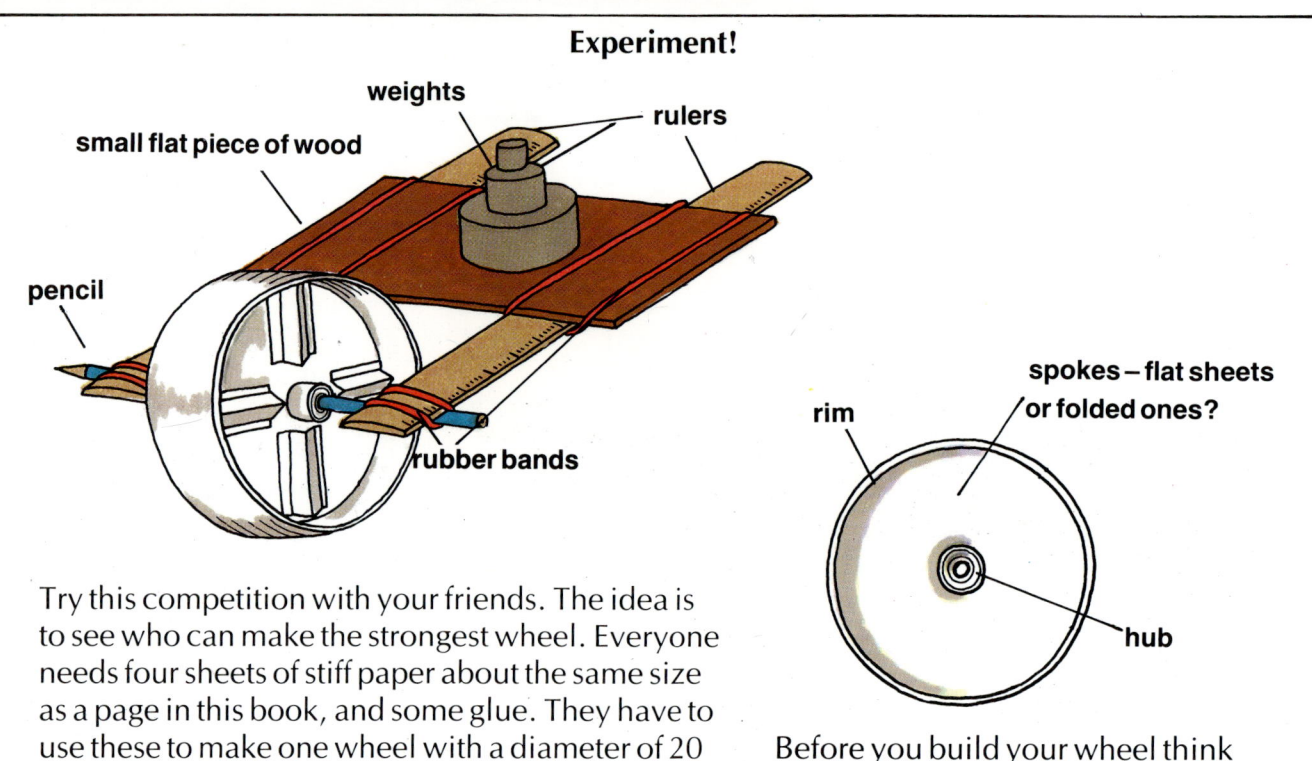

Piston engines

Cars, trucks, motorcycles and light aircraft, as well as many trains, are all driven by piston engines. This type of engine uses pistons moving up and down inside cylinders to turn the crankshaft which turns the wheels. The pistons are linked to the crankshaft by rods connected to cranks on the shaft. The cranks are turned by the piston and rods in the same way as a bicycle pedal is turned by a foot.

Nowadays nearly all piston engines are internal combustion engines. This means that they burn or 'combust' fuel inside the engine. The fuel, mixed with air, explodes inside the cylinder to make the piston move. In cars and aircraft the fuel used is usually petrol. Trucks and trains have a slightly different type of engine, the diesel, which burns a heavier kind of oil.

▽ This is a cutaway model of a car engine. It has four cylinders which fire one after the other to keep the crankshaft turning smoothly. Single cylinder engines, such as those used in small motorbikes, run roughly with a lot of noise and vibration.

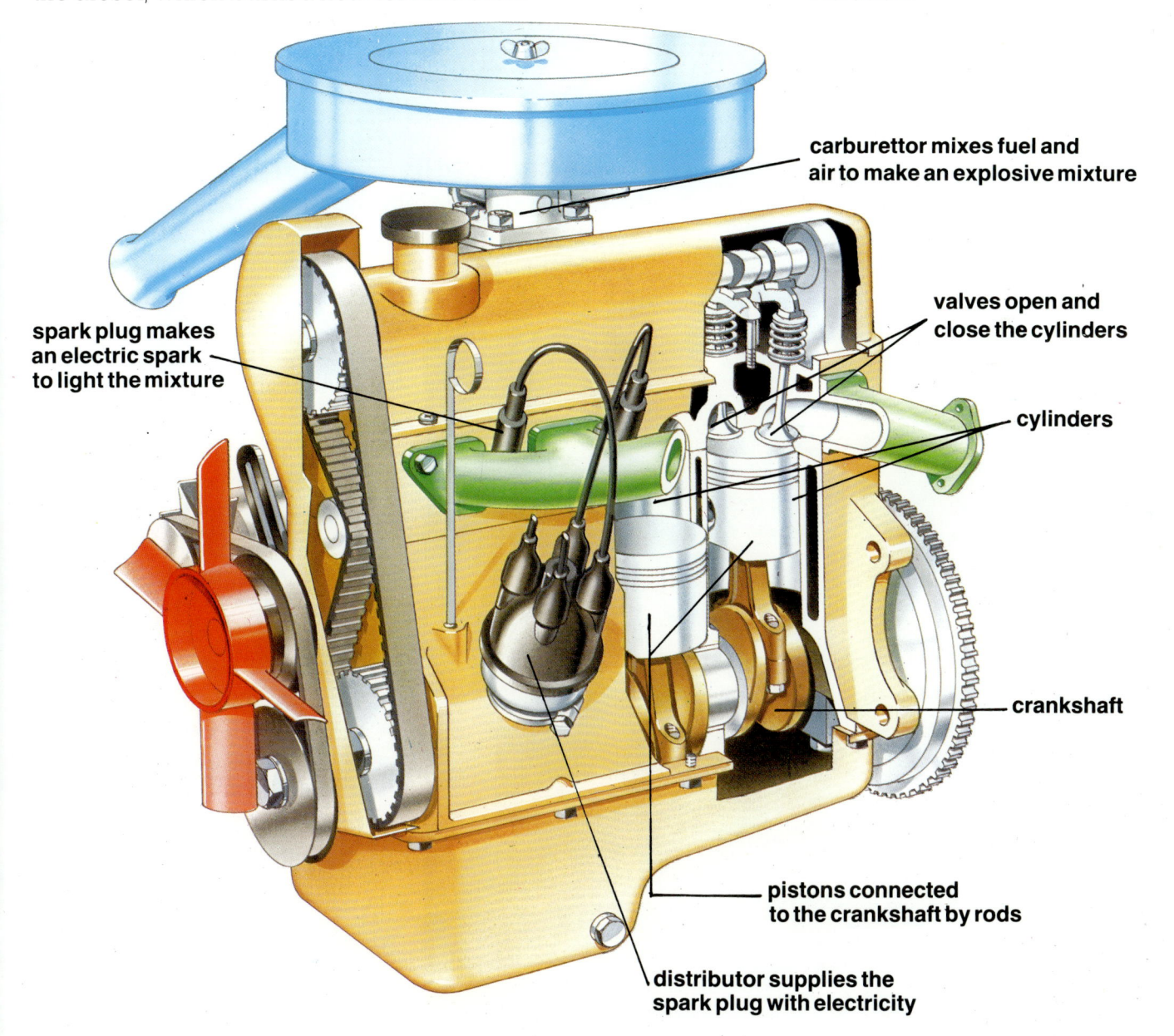

carburettor mixes fuel and air to make an explosive mixture

spark plug makes an electric spark to light the mixture

valves open and close the cylinders

cylinders

crankshaft

pistons connected to the crankshaft by rods

distributor supplies the spark plug with electricity

How cylinders create power

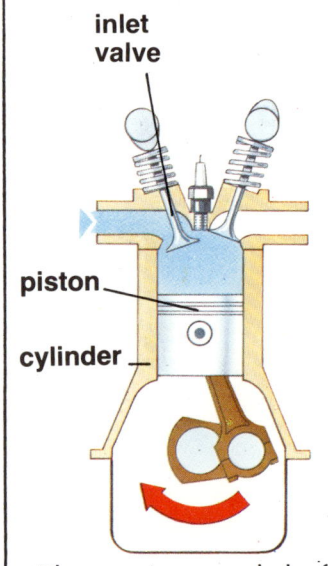

inlet valve — **piston** — **cylinder**

spark plug

exhaust valve

The turning crankshaft pulls the piston down to suck in fuel mixture through the open inlet valve.

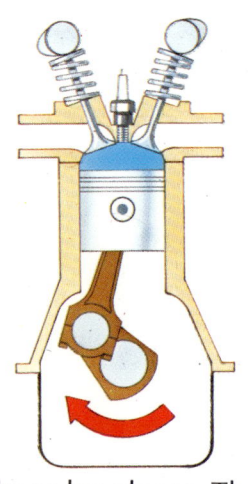

The valve closes. The piston rises to squeeze the mixture so it will explode better.

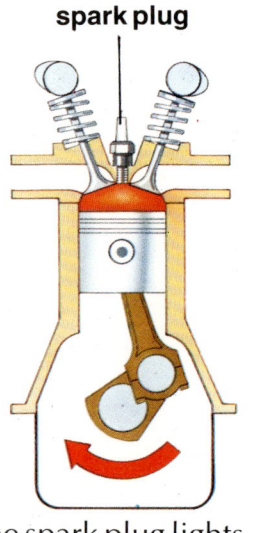

The spark plug lights the mixture which explodes, pushing the piston down to turn the crankshaft.

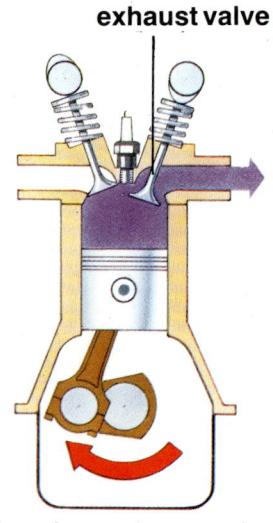

The piston rises again to force the used gases out through the open exhaust valve.

◁ Internal combustion engines can be huge or tiny. This is one of two fairly large ones used in a pilot boat-tug. It is a 250 horse power diesel engine which uses a different way of lighting the fuel than that of an ordinary petrol engine. The fuel mixture is squeezed until it becomes so hot that it catches fire and explodes. The same heating can be felt in a bicycle pump. When it is pumped the air is compressed and the pump gets hot. Diesel engines are often started by an electrically heated 'glow plug'. This works like a spark plug until the engine is running smoothly. It can then be turned off.

▷ The Rolls Royce 'Silver Ghost' was built in 1907 and was very advanced for its time. Most other cars were noisy, smelly and uncomfortable and always breaking down. The Silver Ghost's piston engine was much quieter – so much so you could hardly even hear it coming. Its six cylinders also fired so smoothly that you could balance a coin on its radiator while the engine was running.

◁ Custom cars are built for fun and for showing off. The engine is for looking at as much as the body. Much of this one has been chrome plated.

Steam engines

Over a hundred years ago, most of the power used in the western world came from steam engines. They were used on railways and, when fixed to the spot, in factories where they provided the power for all sorts of machinery. There even used to be steam driven buses. Nowadays most steam engines have been replaced by newer kinds.

Why use steam engines?

Steam engines have many advantages. They are simple to build and easy to look after. They can be run on almost any kind of fuel – coal, wood, oil or even rubbish. They can also be made as big and powerful as is wanted.

But there are disadvantages too. Steam engines use a lot of fuel which makes them expensive to run. They also have to be kept filled up with water the whole time. This is easy to do if the engine is fixed to the spot but it causes problems if it moves. Steam locomotives have to carry a trailer or tender containing tons of water behind them. Steam cars had to keep stopping for water.

The way a steam engine works is simple. A fire, fed by whatever fuel is being used, heats water in a boiler to make steam. The hotter it gets, the greater the pressure of steam in the boiler. Pipes lead the steam from here to a cylinder in which a piston is pushed forward by the force of the steam. This movement opens a valve so that the steam escapes and the piston moves back. The backward and forward action of the piston delivers power to the machinery.

Different types of steam engine

In some more advanced engines the steam is superheated so that it gives extra power. This is done by heating the steam for a second time, after it leaves the boiler. In other engines steam is used to push both sides of the piston. Pistons move within a cylinder and some engines have two or three of these. The steam works one cylinder and then goes to another. This one will be larger because the steam has expanded in the first cylinder. From there it can be piped to a third, even larger, cylinder. Reusing steam means it produces as much energy as possible.

▷ This is an old steam roller shown at work in India. The weight of its engine and wheels helps flatten the road. It can be made heavier still by filling the rolling wheels with water. Real steam rollers like this used to be quite common. But these days most so called 'steam' rollers in fact have a diesel engine.

Key
1 cab
2 firebox
3 boiler
4 firetubes
5 steam chest
6 steam pipe
7 cylinder
8 valve gear
9 driving wheels
10 exhaust pipe
11 smoke box
12 superheater
13 chimney
14 buffers

How a steam locomotive works
◁ A coal fire burns in the firebox in front of the cab. Heat from the fire passes through the walls of the firebox into the surrounding water. More heat passes to the water as the hot gases from the fire pass forward in tubes through the boiler barrel to the smoke box. The heat turns water into steam which is collected and passed through the regulator, a valve controlled from the cab. It is further heated in the superheater before going into the steam chests of two pairs of cylinders. Here it is controlled by valves so that it goes to each end of each cylinder in turn, driving the pistons back and forth. The pistons are connected by rods to cranks which turn the driving wheels.

◁ This type of steam engine was once widely used in all sorts of industry. It is called a 'beam engine' because of the large beam at the top. The cylinder stands under one end of the beam and the piston is connected to the beam. As the piston moves up and down the beam rocks. From the other end of the beam hangs a rod which is connected to pumps or to a crank to turn the factory machinery.

▷ This Foden steam wagon was built in 1922. At that time trucks driven by petrol engines could not be made very large and diesel-engined lorries had not been introduced. So all the big, heavy loads had to be moved in steam trucks which ran on coal. They were powerful and reliable and were used right up until the war in 1939.

Turbines and fans

Fans and turbines are the same sort of machine but they do different jobs and work in different ways. A fan is turned by a motor to blow air while a turbine is turned by air, gas or water flowing through it. Water wheels turned by a stream and windmills turned by the wind are both simple turbines. The more complicated turbines used today are specially designed for the particular work they have to do. They are often part of a larger piece of machinery which also includes a fan.

Different types of turbine

Some turbines are shaped like windmills but instead of vanes they have lots of small blades. These turn inside a tube which keeps the flow going through the turbine straight. Jet engines have turbines like this. They are found at the back of the engine and are turned by the blast of gas created as the engine burns fuel. The spinning turbine drives a compressor which pulls air into the engine to make it work more efficiently.

Turboprops, turboshafts and gas turbines

In certain types of jet engine the turbine may also drive a propellor. Some aircraft have 'turboprop' engines like this while 'turboshaft' engines, in which the turbine drives a rotor, are sometimes used in helicopters. When a jet engine is used on the ground to generate electricity, or in a ship, it is called a gas turbine. Some jet engines are used both in aircraft and, when modified, on the ground.

Water turbines are a rather different shape. One kind has only a few blades and looks like a ship's propeller. It is turned by water running through it, perhaps rushing down from a dam.

△ This is the enormous engine of a Boeing 747 jumbo jet. It contains both a fan and a turbine but this view shows the fan only. The turbine drives the fan which blows air backwards around the outside of the engine so that it mixes with the exhaust blast at the back. This makes the engine work more efficiently at low speeds. The turbine itself is turned by the exhaust blast. Engines like this are called 'fan jets'.

▷ This is a gas turbine engine which is used to drive an electricity generator. You can see what it looks like inside in the cutaway picture at the top of the next page.

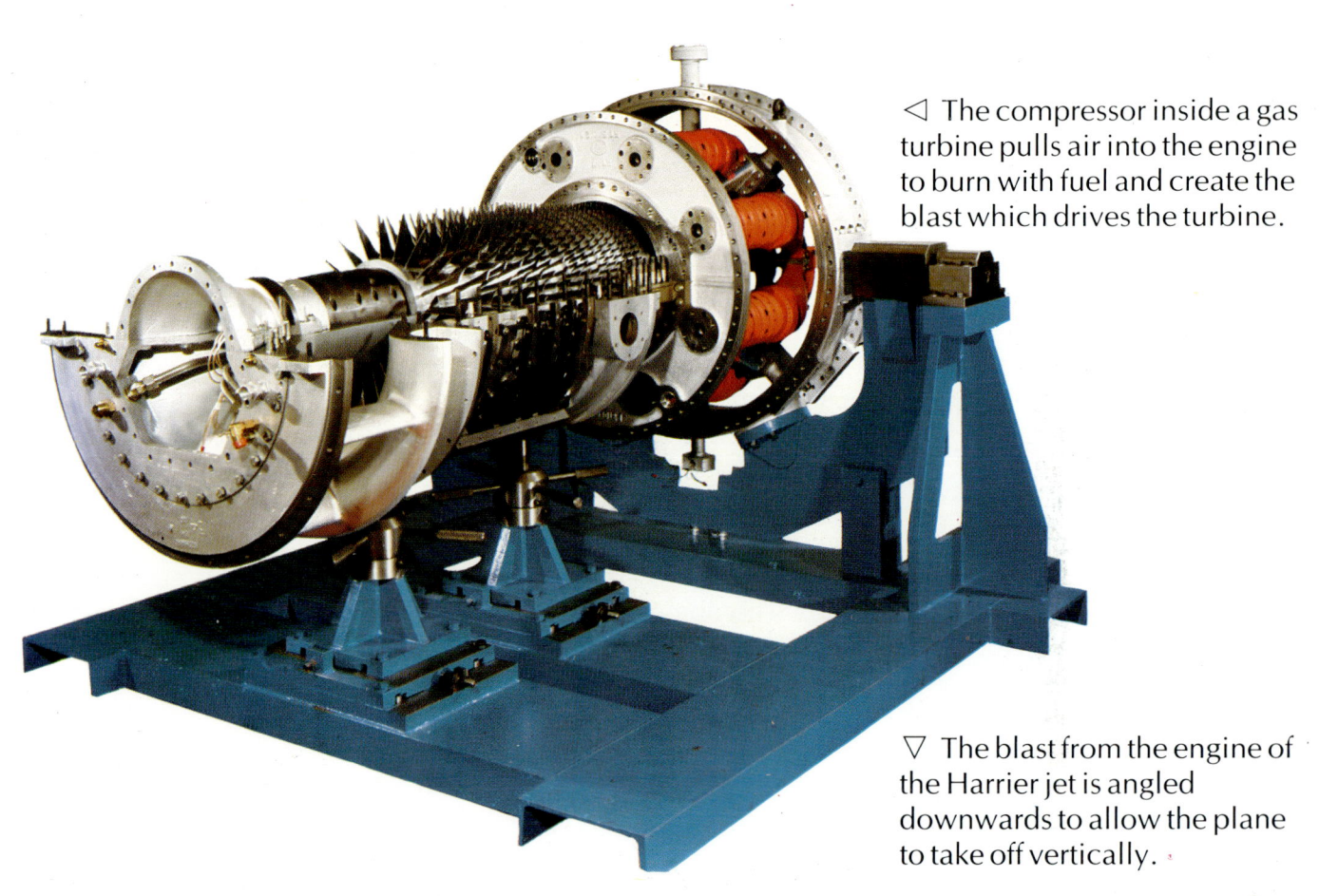

◁ The compressor inside a gas turbine pulls air into the engine to burn with fuel and create the blast which drives the turbine.

▽ The blast from the engine of the Harrier jet is angled downwards to allow the plane to take off vertically.

▷ This powerful Bentley, built in 1930, has a supercharger. You can see its casing just behind the number plate. The supercharger works by blowing extra air into the engine's cylinders so that more fuel can be burnt. This makes the car nearly twice as powerful as it would be without it. The supercharger is placed where it is because it is turned by a shaft on the front of the engine.

◁ Instead of a supercharger driven by a shaft, a modern engine may have a turbocharger like this one. It is the same as a supercharger but is driven by a turbine spun by the exhaust gases of the engine flowing through it. The spinning turbine turns a fan which blows air into the engine so that the fuel burns more efficiently. You can see the turbine on the left while the blower is on the right. Turbochargers are used to give extra power to racing cars. Some of the fastest ordinary cars and many vehicles with diesel engines also have one.

Electric motors

Electric motors come in all sorts of shapes and sizes. The largest ones, such as those used in steel mills, may be as much as six metres tall while the smallest watch motors are no bigger than a pill. They work at different rates too. Some turn once a second or even slower, others move at tens of thousands of times that speed. Exact timing is particularly important for motors in things like record players and clocks. They simply would not work properly if the motor turned at the wrong speed.

'Secondary' machines

An electric motor is not the same sort of machine as the engines we have already looked at in this book. It does not burn fuel itself but uses power from either a battery or mains electricity. The other engines all created their own power by burning fuel themselves. Because of this engineers call them 'prime movers'. Prime means first. Electric motors and any other machines which use power from a prime mover are called 'secondary' machines.

How an electric motor works

The heart of an electric motor is an electromagnet. This is a magnet made of coils of wire that become magnetic when an electric current passes through them. When the current is on the magnet pulls, when it is switched off it stops pulling. The pull created by this magnetic attraction is what makes the motor move. The exact way in which this happens depends on the sort of electric motor and on how it is arranged.

◁ An electric motor gives a lot of power for its size. You can start and stop it just by moving a switch, it is always clean and does not produce poisonous exhaust fumes. So it is ideal for driving machines like this borer, in use in a metal workshop.

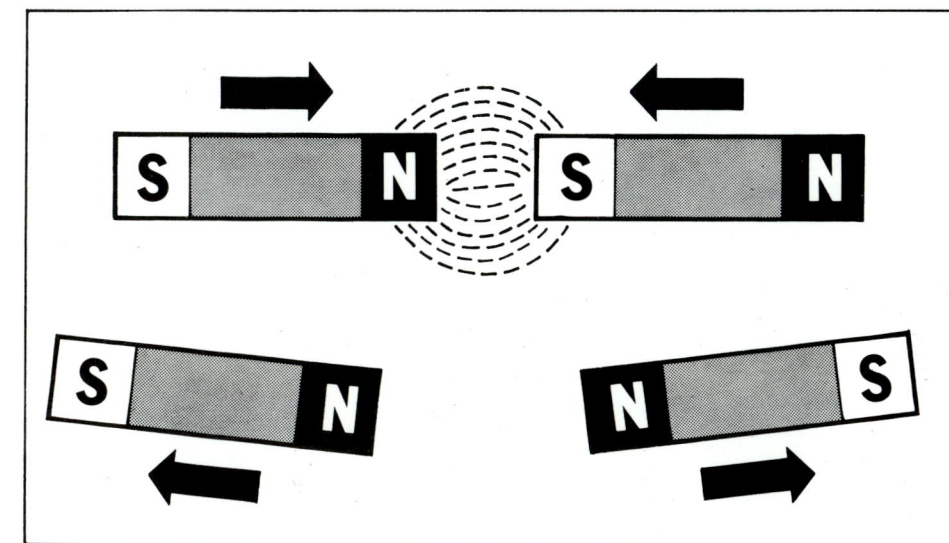

Magnets
A magnet attracts pieces of iron towards it. It has two ends, the 'north' and 'south poles'. A north pole attracts the south pole of another magnet but pushes away another north pole. Permanent magnets made of solid metal work all the time. Electromagnets, made from coils of wire, can be switched on and off.

When an electromagnet is switched on, the magnetic attraction it exerts will pull something a short way in one direction. It will not make the thing spin, which is what is needed to make the motor work. In order to get this to happen, the turning part of the motor, called the rotor, has to be arranged so that it turns a certain distance every time it is pulled by the magnet.

In the simplest kind of motor the rotor is pulled halfway round. But mains electric current flows one way and then stops and flows the other way 50 times a second. So the rotor is pulled halfway and then the current is reversed so that it pulls the other way, making the rotor return to its starting position. Because the rotor is already half way it does not turn back but continues around the circle to get back that way. This is what makes it spin.

So long as the current keeps being reversed, the rotor keeps going round and round. Battery-powered motors have devices which reverse the current.

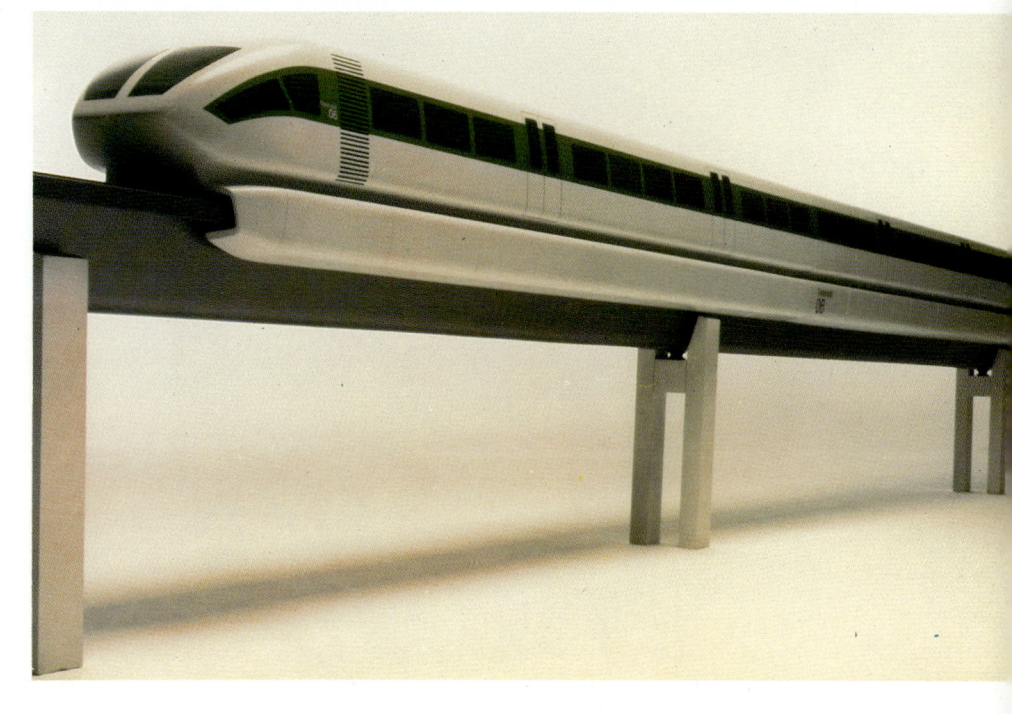

▷ This is a model of a new train being tested in Germany. There is already a real one like it working in Birmingham in England. It has no wheels but is raised just above the track when it runs. The train is pulled by a linear motor. This is just like an ordinary electric motor with its parts 'unrolled' into a straight line. The train is held up by magnetic force.

How a battery electric motor works

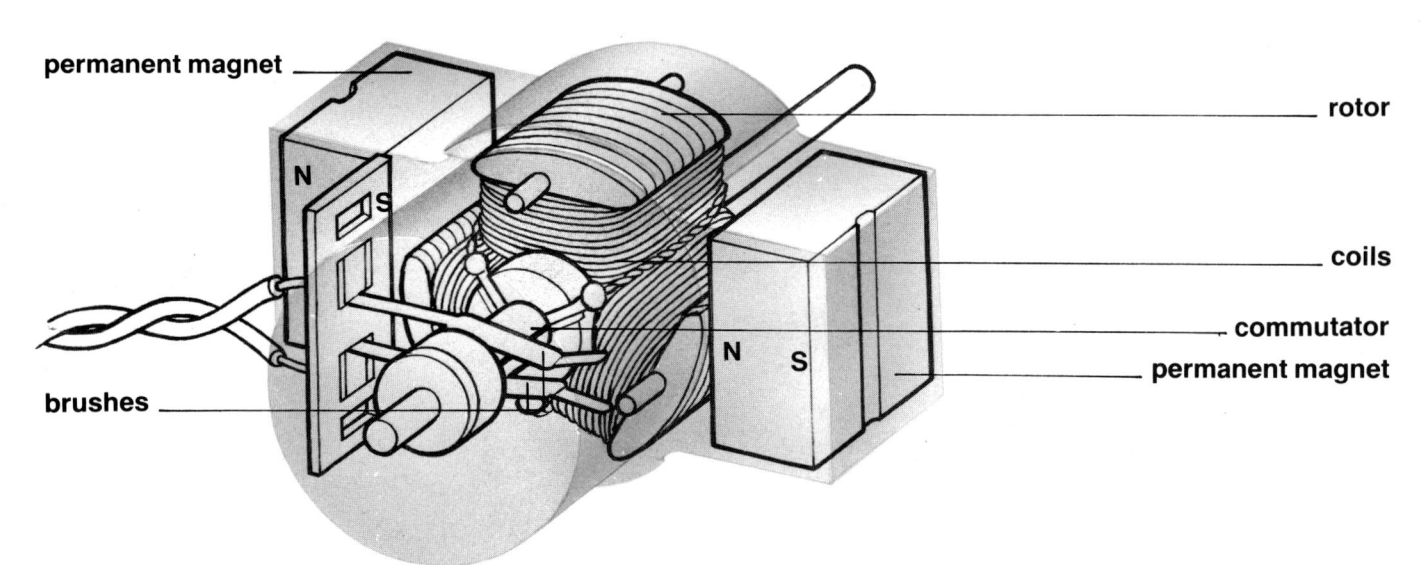

△ This small motor powers a toy. It is driven by batteries which give a steady electric current flowing in one direction. They send current through the brushes, which touch the metal pieces on the commutator. From here current goes to the coils of the rotor. That makes the rotor become an electromagnet. The rotor sits between two permanent iron magnets. The magnetism makes the rotor turn to bring its north pole next to the south pole of a permanent magnet. The commutator turns too, so it switches the current to flow the other way in the coils. That pulls the rotor the other way, making it turn full circle.

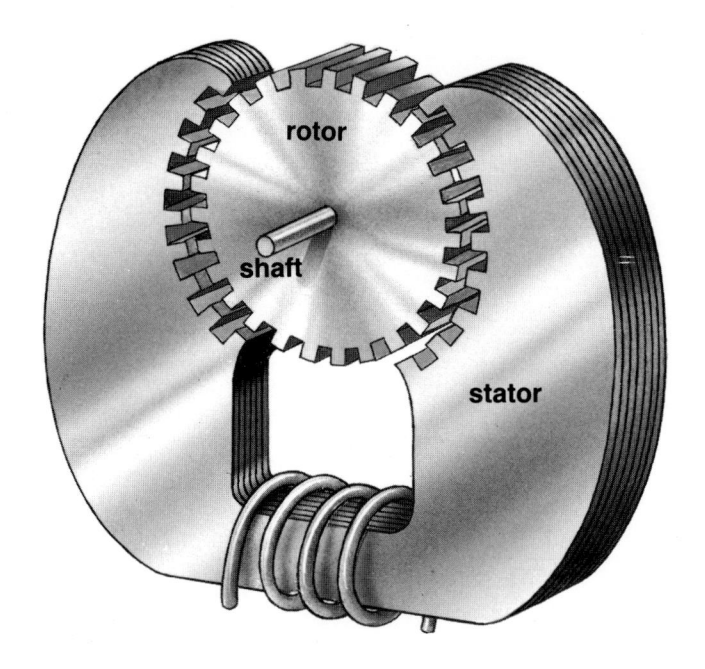

◁ This diagram shows how an electric clock works. The stator does not move and is an electromagnet. The rotor turns and in doing so turns a shaft which moves the hands of the clock. The stator and rotor both have teeth which do not quite touch. Electricity creates the magnetism which pulls the two sets of teeth together. In order to start the clock, the electricity has to be turned on. Mains electric current flows one way and then stops and flows the other way 50 times a second. Each time the current is reversed, the rotor moves.

Conveyors, pipelines, cableways

Conveyors, pipelines and cableways all provide ways of moving large quantities of goods or people from place to place quickly and easily. Simple kinds of them have been in use for a long time. Waterpipes have been found in the ruins of several of the world's oldest cities, built thousands of years ago.

In the Middle Ages a very basic cableway was used at Salzburg castle in Austria. People got so tired of carrying heavy loads up the steep hill to the castle that they built a wooden track. Ropes were used to haul trucks up the track to the top.

The first railways pulled by cable were built in the mountains of Switzerland in the 1880s. There were two cars connected by a huge cable which ran around a big wheel at the top. As they moved, the weight of one car balanced the weight of the other. Apart from in the middle where the cars passed each other, it was a single track. In the middle, cars were automatically switched to left or right tracks. Cable railways like this are often called 'funicular' railways.

Ski lifts and escalators

Overhead cableways have been used to carry buckets of ore at mines for centuries. The first to carry people was built in Switzerland in 1908. Since then, ski lifts of many kinds have been designed and most resorts have one or more. The first escalators were made in New York and Paris in the 1890s. The idea for them came from conveyor belts used to carry goods. The earliest kinds even looked a bit like a conveyor belt since they did not have steps. They were just a moving ramp and because of this could only be built on a shallow slope.

△ This machine both carries and freezes peas. It is a type of conveyor belt. The peas travel along a trough with holes in the bottom. A blast of chilled air is blown through the holes, lifting the peas so that they flow easily. At the same time they freeze without sticking to each other, so they can be easily packed in bags.

◁ This pipeline carries oil thousands of miles across Alaska. It is raised on stilts to stop it melting the frozen ground and sinking in. The stilts have to be high enough to let caribou deer like this go underneath. They travel across Alaska twice a year and the pipeline crosses their path. Since the deer refused to use bridges to get over it, stilts were the best answer to the problem.

Conveyor belts and cables are both supported by wheels. Because of this they cannot be made more than a few kilometres long. Beyond this there is so much friction in the large number of wheels needed that the machine will not move.

When things like coal have to be sent long distances they are usually carried by train. But oil can be sent any distance by pipeline. Now engineers have found a way of sending coal by pipeline too. It is crushed into small pieces no more than two centimetres across. These are then mixed with water to make a gritty sludge which flows along the pipe quite easily. At the far end it is poured out and left to dry.

Another unlikely product which can be carried in a pipe is grain. Large pipes are used to load and unload ships carrying grain, and to take it to stores. Cylinder-like objects called 'pigs' are sent down pipelines to clean them and to separate flows of different products.

▷ A travelator carrying passengers at Charles de Gaulle airport in Paris. A travelator is a sort of conveyor belt that runs on rollers. This one has been built inside a tube to keep passengers dry as they move from building to building at the airport.

◁ This is a cabin lift in use at a ski resort. It is one of many kinds of cableways used by skiers. Some lifts have several small cabins or chairs which carry a couple of people each. Others may have cabins large enough to hold 50 or 100 passengers. Ski tows run on cables which are much closer to the ground. They carry hangers which the skiers lean against as they are pulled along the snow to the top of the slope.

Any machine which carries people must be safe. Escalators have to be designed so that it is nearly impossible to get your feet or hands trapped. Rubber strips guard the edges and the steps have ridges on them to stop people slipping. At the end of the escalator is a plate with teeth which fit between the ridges so that nothing can get past. Just in case something does happen, there are switches at the top and bottom which can stop the escalator in seconds. Overhead cableways also have to be made as safe as possible. They can be stopped if any car starts to sway dangerously. If the motor breaks down the cars can be wound along by hand.

▷ This is a conveyor belt used to carry the ore from a diamond mine in Angola. You have to dig out huge amounts of ore to find one diamond. Mining here is done over a wide area, so the ore often has to be carried a long way to the extracting plant which finds the diamonds.

Ships and boats

Anything large enough that floats can work as a boat. Many materials have been used to make boats in different parts of the world. The simplest kind is a log raft made of tree trunks tied together. Rafts like this are unsinkable and can be strong enough to use on the open sea. Indians from Peru once sailed along the coast of South America on large rafts made of light balsa wood. Where there are no good trees, other things can be used. In central Africa and Bolivia they make rafts out of reeds tied into a boat shape. In India goat skins are sewn up and filled with air to make floats for crossing rivers.

Other simple types of boat

Dugout canoes are another simple kind of boat. They are made from hollowed-out tree trunks carved into shape. The Inuit (who used to be called Eskimos) do not use dugouts like this because they live in the Arctic where there are no trees. Instead they make canoes out of seal skins stretched over a frame of thin wood. Westerners have borrowed the shape of the boat and its name, kayak, for sports canoes. Skin boats were also once made in Wales and Ireland. North American Indians even used to make canoes covered in birch bark. But most boats were made from strips of wood joined together until the first iron ships were built over 150 years ago.

▽ All normal ships and boats are roughly the same shape – long with pointed ends. This shape cuts through the water well but it can be improved by making small changes. The fastest ships are narrow, with curved sides and a sharp bow at the front. An aircraft carrier, like all warships, has to be very fast. Under its odd-shaped landing deck it has the long, sleek shape shown in this outline drawing.

▷ Cargo ships such as container ships like this do not have to move very quickly. It is more important that there is plenty of room on board for storing cargo. All the holds have to have neat rectangular shapes that make them easy to pack with containers or goods. This is why cargo ships usually have straight sides, pointed only at the very end.

▷ Speedboats go so fast that most of their hull or body is forced out of the water. Only a little triangle at the stern touches the water. This means that there is very little friction between the boat and the water at high speeds.

Small canoes and rafts are pushed along with paddles. The two-ended kayak paddle is very efficient. Larger boats need oars to move them. These are fixed to the edge of the boat by a pivot which allows them to turn freely.

All over the world people have invented sails of different shapes. When sailing boats do not have the wind straight behind them they are blown slightly sideways. Sometimes they lean over so far that they capsize. The keel was invented to stop this happening. It is a deep ridge on the bottom of the boat which keeps it moving straight through the water and helps it to stay upright. The people of the Indian Ocean and Pacific islands made their boats more stable by inventing the outrigger. This is a long float fixed to arms which stick out on one side of the boat. Catamarans work in a similar way. Their two narrow hulls balance each other so that they are fairly stable even in strong winds.

The first boats to be driven by steam were built in the early 1800s. Now engine-powered boats are used almost everywhere in the world. Modern small boats have petrol engines while larger ones use diesel. Full-sized ships may be driven by diesels or by steam turbines.

What is the difference between a boat and a ship? Nowadays it is just a matter of size but in the days of sail 'ship' had an exact meaning. A ship then had three or more masts carrying only square sails. The small, triangular jib sails at the bows and other small sails were not counted. If it had other kinds of sails it was not a ship, no matter how big it was.

Modern ships can be amazingly large. The biggest oil tankers weigh half a million tonnes and the crew have to use tricycles to get about. Bicycles would be impossible to balance if the sea was rough. The longest boats need warning of several kilometres to change direction.

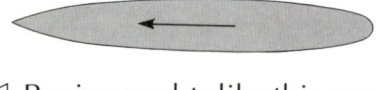

◁ Racing yachts like this one have long, narrow hulls which taper at the end. You can see their shape at the waterline in the drawing above. It is streamlined to help the boat go as fast as possible. Catamarans and trimarans go faster still with two or three very slim hulls. Viking ships used to have the same tapering shape and were famous for the speed at which they moved.

◁ Another boat with the narrow, pointed shape that gives speed is the kayak. Modern kayaks are based on the design of those built by the Inuit. They are made out of plastic strengthened by glass and moulded to shape.

Sails, propellors, wings, rotors

The wings of birds and aircraft, the sails of boats and windmills, the propellors of aircraft and ships and the rotors of helicopters all work in the same way. They create 'lift'. This is a pressure which pushes upwards. It is used to keep things in the air or to make them move in certain ways.

Wings, sails, propellors and rotors all have one side that curves outwards and one that is flat or curves slightly inwards. When air flows over the curved side its pressure drops below the pressure of the air next to the flatter surface. Because the pressure is higher beneath it pushes upwards, so creating lift.

Differences in pressure

The difference in pressure happens because of the way air flows over the two surfaces. Air going the longer way round, over the curved surface, has to flow faster to join up with the air which has gone straight past the flat side. As it speeds up its pressure drops. Air from below, where the pressure is normal, is attracted towards the area of low pressure. This is why it pushes upwards.

Aircraft wings and helicopter rotors are arranged so that the curve is on top. This means that the lift that is created pushes upwards to keep them in the air. A propellor is curved on the front so the lift pushes it forwards. Boat sails also bulge towards the front so the lift they create pushes the boat forward. Birds can create more or less lift by holding their wings at different angles. They need lots of lift to takeoff but less when they are flying along.

▽ All flying birds use their wings to create lift. Most also use them like oars to 'row' through the air. But albatrosses like this one hardly ever flap their wings. They can fly just above the sea for days, even flying in their sleep. Gentle currents of air pushed up by sea waves stop the bird dropping as it glides forwards.

The person who discovered that fast flowing streams of air have low pressure was a Swiss mathematician called Daniel Bernoulli. That is why the discovery is called the 'Bernoulli effect'. Daniel first worked it out while experimenting with water. This also has low pressure when it flows fast. The ship's propellor on the opposite page and the hydrofoil below both show the Bernoulli effect working in water.

△ Wings are not always used to lift things. Racing cars have them at the front and back. Their wings are upside down. This means that they push the car down into the road when it is going fast so that the car tyres grip better.

◁ A hydrofoil is a wing that goes through water. This boat is 'flying' on hydrofoils. You cannot see them because they are just below the surface of the water. The boat's hull is lifted up so there is little friction between it and the water.

An aircraft has to fly above a certain speed to get enough lift to keep it in the air. This is because the lift comes from air flowing fast over the aircraft's wings. If the plane's speed drops too much the aircraft will stall. When this happens it suddenly drops through the air. In order to get out of the stall the pilot has to increase the aircraft's speed again.

Helicopter rotors turn at a steady speed so the air flows over them at a steady speed too. This means that they create a steady amount of lift. Helicopters can hover because of this. To make them climb, the rotor blades are tilted to create extra lift.

Boats get lift from their sails. These can be moved around to get as much wind in them as possible. Boats can sail across the wind or even slightly towards it if their sails are at the right angle. When they zig-zag across it they are said to be 'tacking'. But they can also be steered 'too close to the wind', too near to the direction the wind is coming from. When this happens the sail flaps wildly and the boat suddenly slows down. On a large sailing ship this can break the mast.

◁ This is a boat propellor being tested in a tank of water. You can see how it is throwing water backwards. This is happening because the propellor is fixed in place to stop it moving forwards.

The Bernoulli effect

When air flows over a curved surface it speeds up. This makes its pressure fall. The higher pressure of the air below the surface pushes up to create lift.

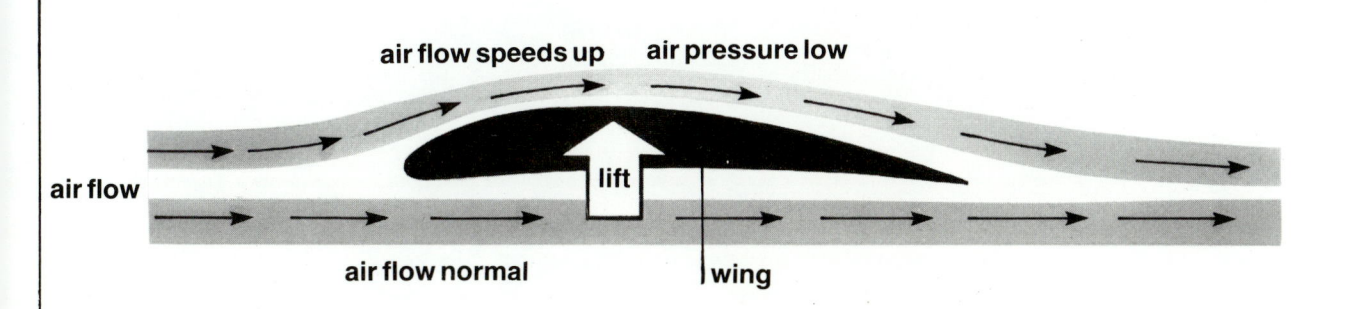

How animals and helicopters fly

Birds, bats and insects fly in the same sort of way as helicopters. They use their wings both to lift them up and to make them go forwards. Helicopters use their rotor blades to do the same things.

Birds and bats move their wings in the same way. Each wing flaps down and forwards, then up and backwards. As it goes down, the wing is higher at the front than it is at the back. It creates lift like an aircraft wing, keeping the bird in the air. When the wing is pulled up again it is held vertically. It sweeps the air backwards like an oar in water. This creates forward thrust to push the bird forward.

How insects fly

Insects fly differently. Their flat wings do not create lift in the same way as a bird's curved ones do. The insect brings its wings flat together over its back. Then it separates them, starting with the front edge of the wing. Air rushes in from the front and sweeps back over the wing as it moves down. The moving air creates low pressure above the wing so that it lifts the insect. It also thrusts it in the other direction, forwards.

Birds and aircraft both use their tails to steer. They also use their wings to tilt themselves. Bats and insects have to use their wings alone because they do not have tails. They steer by changing the angle at which their wings move through the air.

▷ Helicopters hover in a way in which ordinary aircraft never could. As you can see here they can stay still enough for troops to leap out safely. Because of this they are also used to rescue people out of the sea or lift them from boats to the shore. Sometimes helicopters are even used to film events for television.

▽ This photograph was taken at a very high speed to show how a lacewing moves its wings. You can see clearly how it brings them down and then strikes them together again over its back. All insects fly in this way.

The rotor blades of a helicopter create lift in the same way as aircraft wings. They spin at the same speed all the time. This does not change even if the helicopter is hovering or climbing instead of moving forwards. The amount of lift the rotor blades create can be increased by tilting the front edge of each blade up. This makes the helicopter climb. To make it go forward, the whole rotor has to be tilted forwards. This is done by making each blade in turn tilt as it goes around the back of its circle. The blade flattens out again when it comes round to the front. The diagrams on the next page show this happening. The rotor can also be tilted backwards or to the side. This makes the helicopter fly backwards or sideways.

Tail rotors

The spin of the rotor tends to make the body of the helicopter spin in the opposite direction. To stop this happening, there is a small tail rotor which creates a sideways thrust. Its blades can also be tilted so that the tail swings to the right or left.

Some of the largest helicopters have two main rotors. These spin in opposite directions so there is no pull on the helicopter's body. They do not need the small tail rotor to help balance the machine. Helicopters like this are used by the army to move large numbers of troops and equipment.

How a helicopter flies

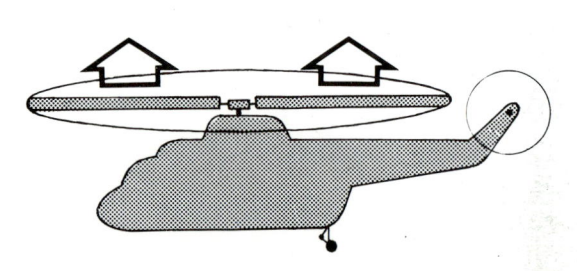

The front and back of the rotor create equal lift when the helicopter is hovering. The tail rotor balances the spin created by the main rotor. So the helicopter's body stays still.

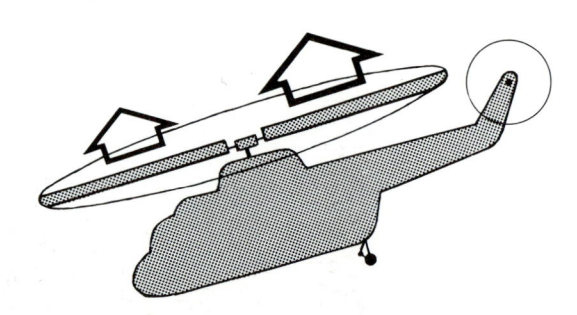

The rotor blades are tilted up at the back of the circle to make the helicopter go forward. This creates more lift at the back so that the whole rotor tilts.

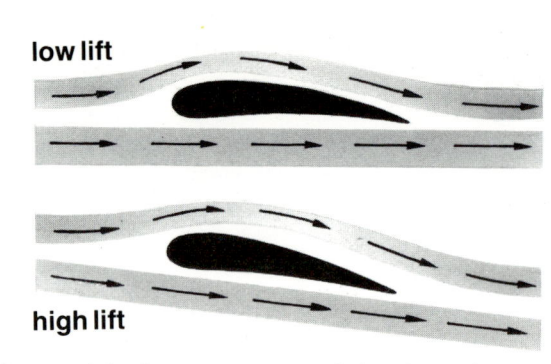

low lift

high lift

Tilting a blade increases its lift. The pilot controls the tilt over all the circle of the rotor with the collective pitch lever. The cyclic pitch lever controls the tilt of the blades over part of the circle.

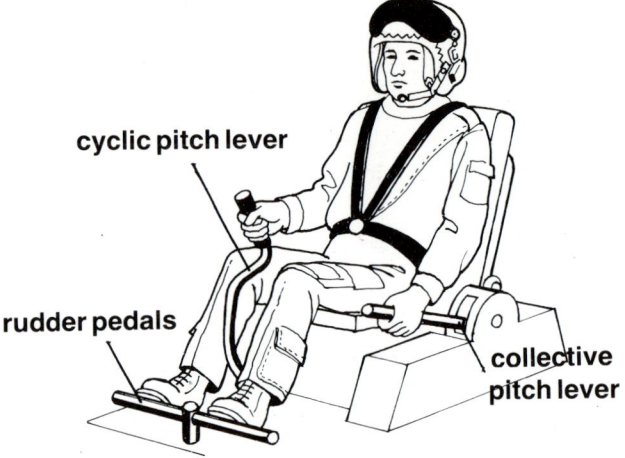

The pilot holds one lever in each hand. He uses the rudder pedals to control the tilt of the tail rotor blades.

Make a toy helicopter!

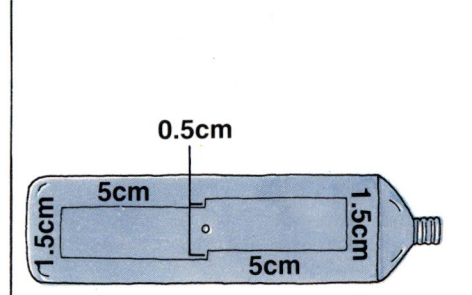

Cut the rotor from a small, straight-sided plastic bottle. Make a hole in the centre.

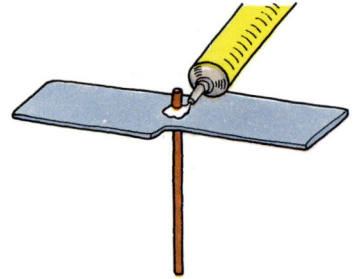

Glue the rotor firmly to a round stick. Something like a toffee apple stick will do.

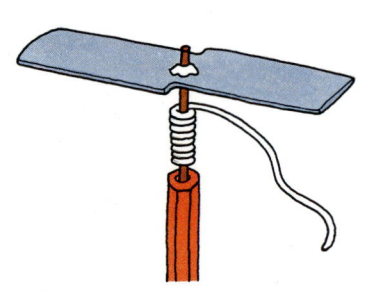

Launch it from an empty ballpoint case by winding round and pulling a string.

Aircraft and gliders

Helicopters have blades which spin round, but most ordinary planes have fixed wings. They are often called 'fixed wing' aircraft because of this. The engines drive the plane forward so that all the wings do is create lift. Gliding is a form of fixed wing flying without an engine. Some birds and animals glide and any aircraft can do it if its engine is turned off. Special gliders are built and flown for sport.

To keep flying level or to climb, an aircraft needs power. A glider goes forward because it is diving through the air all the time. It has long, thin wings which cause little drag from air friction. A very well built glider will drop less than one metre for every 50 metres it goes forward.

Thermals

Gliders start their flight by being towed up by an ordinary plane. Sometimes a winch on the ground is used instead and the glider is attached to it by a cable. Once up, the pilot looks for 'thermals'. These are places where the air is rising in a strong upward current caused by warm land beneath. The movement of this rising air is faster than that of the falling glider, so it makes the glider rise. When the pilot reaches the top of one thermal he has to find and reach another before the glider drops too far.

On a warm day when there are lots of thermals around a glider can travel thousands of kilometres. The only thing that stops it is nightfall. When the Sun goes down the ground cools and the thermals stop rising. The glider pilot on a record-breaking run must quickly find somewhere to land.

△ This aircraft, a Tornado, shows that on some planes 'fixed wings' are not completely fixed all the time. The wings of a Tornado can be moved. For takeoff and landing they are stretched out sideways to create the most lift at low speed. For high speed flight they are pivoted back to reduce drag.

◁ You can see the long, narrow wings of the glider quite clearly here. Wings and body are smooth and streamlined to reduce friction as it glides through the air.

▷ Flying dragons are one of the few types of animal, apart from birds, that can glide. Their long tails help them stay balanced.

▽ The wings of frigate birds are a similar shape to the glider's. They allow the birds to soar gracefully through the air using very little energy.

Some birds also use thermals. They are called 'soaring' birds and their kind of flight is known as soaring. Birds of this type have long wings which the designers of gliders copied. The wings are very efficient but even so the birds sometimes have to flap them. They have to do this on takeoff or when they cannot find a thermal to carry them upwards.

A few animals glide, although they cannot soar like birds. They have wide flaps of skin which act as wings. The flying dragon you can see above is like this, and so are some squirrels and frogs. There is even a very flat snake which can glide. The distances these animals cover in this way are fairly short. The movement is closer to a controlled drop than to real flight. The best of these gliding animals is the flying fish, which uses its long fins as wings. When it is chased it swims very fast, then bursts out of the water and glides many metres.

Parachuting

Parachuting is another kind of controlled drop. The large surface of the parachute means that it meets a lot of air resistance as it moves downwards. This slows the fall. A skilled parachutist can even glide. By pulling the cords of his chute he can slip sideways through the air. The chute will begin to act like a glider because the air flowing sideways over the curved top creates lift. A good parachutist can steer his chute to land at an exact spot but he may hit the ground quite hard.

△ This parachutist is pulling the cords of his chute to make it move forwards or sideways, so that he can steer closer to the landing site.

Bird shapes and movements

The shape of a bird tells us a great deal about the way it flies and lives. Birds which glide and soar have the largest wings. Albatrosses are like this. Their long, thin wings create a lot of lift. They also cut cleanly through the air so that there is little resistance or drag. This means that the bird can glide just above the sea for quite some time. Albatrosses hardly ever flap their wings. If they had to they would soon tire because their wings are so long, with a span of 3.5 metres or more.

Soaring birds

Soaring birds which use thermals have wings with a slightly different shape. They are broader and not so long when compared to the size of the bird. An eagle's wings are like this. They allow the bird to turn sharply in the air, which an albatross cannot do. This is useful because the bird often has to turn in a tight circle to stay in the thermal.

The wings of an eagle also have to be very strong because they are used as air brakes. When the bird sees a prey on the ground it folds its wings and drops like a stone. It reaches a very high speed as it falls. Just above the ground the eagle unfolds its wings and brakes hard. Hawks and vultures swoop down on their prey in the same way. Some hawks have been seen diving at speeds of over 200 kilometres per hour. They have to move this fast in order to catch the animal before it has time to escape.

△ The kestrel is a kind of hawk. It can fly very swiftly and very slowly. When it faces into a light wind it can even hover. Kestrels beat their wings quickly with a short movement. The little feather at the front of their wings smooths the air flow over them. This helps them to fly at low speeds.

◁ The wings of an albatross are so long that if it lands on water or flat ground it cannot take off again. The bird nests on cliffs so that it can launch itself into the air easily.

▽ Ostriches are the largest living members of a family of flightless birds found in Africa, South America and Australasia. All this family have long, strong legs and can run fast and far. Their wings are not useless. When the birds get hot from running they spread them out to help them cool down. They also use them as a weapon to attack other animals who threaten them.

Birds which fly at high speed have smaller wings that have a swept-back shape which narrows into a point at the end. Hawks and swifts are like this. The shape of their wings means that they cut through the air very cleanly, causing little drag. Their small size also means that the bird can flap them quickly and use them to turn sharply. Both these birds catch flying prey – hawks eat other birds and swifts eat insects. So they have to be able to move fast in any direction to catch the food they need to survive.

Different wing shapes

Another kind of wing is a short broad one, like a pheasant's. They too can be flapped very quickly to give the bird a fast takeoff from the ground. Pheasants need to be able to do this because they often have to escape from animals which attack them. But their wings are no good for long flights.

Other birds manage to fly thousands of miles when they migrate. The record holder is the Arctic tern which flies from the Arctic to the Antarctic and back every year. Its wings are pointed and streamlined. But other birds which fly over long distances have wings which are shaped differently. Carrier pigeons, for example, have medium-length, medium-width wings with rounded ends. Geese and ducks, which often make long migrations, have straight wings which look oddly small in comparison to the size of their bodies.

Some birds have shapes which actually make it hard for them to fly. The male argus pheasant is one of these. It has a very long tail which attracts the female but makes it almost impossible for the bird to get off the ground. Toucans have huge beaks which are good for eating the soft fruit they like but no help when it comes to flying. Surprisingly they manage it somehow. Other birds now do not fly at all. Usually they have muscular legs for running but small wings. The kiwi bird from New Zealand has the smallest ones. They are completely hidden under its feathers, so that the bird almost looks as though it has no wings at all.

◁ Humming birds are tiny and the only birds that can hover without moving at all. They hang in front of flowers and push in their long beaks so that they can suck out the nectar. When they hover like this they move their wings so fast that you can only see a blur. They beat backwards and forwards rather than up and down, making a complicated figure-of-eight pattern. This keeps them up in the air.

▷ Penguins cannot fly in the air at all but they do use their small wings to 'fly' underwater. They are excellent swimmers and live by hunting fish. Because of this they do not need the strong legs that most other flightless birds have. Penguins walk clumsily, waddling from side to side. If there is ice about they prefer to slide over it on their stomachs, pushing themselves along with their feet at a fair speed.

Other flying creatures

So far we have looked at the flight of birds and of a typical insect but there are many other creatures which also fly. Here we are going to concentrate on insects which fly in different ways.

Dragonflies

Insects likes bees and wasps and the lacewing shown on page 46 have four wings that move up and down together. Dragonflies move their front and back or hind wings in opposite ways, one pair going down while the other goes up. They can fly faster than any other insects, sometimes reaching up to 55 kilometres per hour in short bursts. They are also the only insect which can fly backwards. They are able to do this because they have a rubbery 'spring' at the back of their wing roots. The spring alters the angle of the wings so that when they are moved the dragonfly is pushed backwards rather than forwards.

Flies and beetles

Some insects fly with only one pair of wings. Flies use their front wings. Their hind wings have turned into small sticks with knobbly ends. They move up and down in the opposite direction from the wings, balancing the wing movement so that the fly's flight is smooth and level. Beetles fly with their hind wings only. Their front wings have changed into hard protective cases which cover the hind wings when they are folded. It is these cases which give beetles their 'armoured' look. In flight the cases are opened out stiffly to the sides.

△ Dragonflies are the tigers of the insect world – large, fast and hungry. They dart after other insects and catch them with their feet. Here you can see the dragonfly's two pairs of wings moving independently. This way of flying helps them to move quickly. Dragonflies can be very big. The largest ones we know of these days have a wingspan of nearly 15 centimetres.

Bats are found in most parts of the world. Usually they are small, only about the size of a mouse. But their broad wings tend to make them look bigger. The 'flying fox' bats of Africa, south Asia and Australasia are the largest. They are about as big as a squirrel and their main food is fruit.

Bats' wings

Bats' wings are very different from those of birds. The wing bones of a bird are all at the front edge. Under its feathers, a bird's wing looks like an arm and hand with all the fingers joined together. The main, outer wing feathers stretch back from the 'hand'. The smaller, inner feathers are found closer to the 'forearm'. But bats have four long, thin 'fingers' with skin stretched between them. Another piece of skin attaches the 'little finger' to the side of the bat's body. When bats rest or sleep they hang upside-down, clinging on with the claws of their hind feet. Insect-eating bats catch their prey with these claws. One kind of bat even uses them to seize small fish.

△ This is a flock of 'flying fox' bats photographed in Java. Unlike most small kinds of bat these fly by day. Bats that fly at night find their way in the dark by using a sort of radar. They make high-pitched squeaks and then judge where they are by listening to echoes bouncing back from nearby objects. This is why they have such big ears. Flying foxes rely more on sight when they fly and are not able to hear the echoes quite as well as the night-fliers. No bats are blind – they can all see perfectly well.

Butterflies have four large wings, two at the front and two at the back on either side. The front and back wings overlap and move together. When it flies, the insect brings the wings together over its back and then separates them, keeping them flat. As the wings go down they push down a big eddy of air which forces the insect upwards. You can see the effect of this in a butterfly's flight.

Every time the wings reach the bottom of their flap, the insect rises. As the wings move back, it falls.

This explains why all butterflies flutter as they fly. The fluttering does not mean that they fly badly. Some species, like the American monarch butterfly, migrate over several thousands of kilometres.

▷ This is a cardinal beetle which has got its wing cases open and its wings unfolded ready to fly. The wing cases protect the beetle well when they are shut. But in the air they get in the way and so no beetle can fly very well. Many of the larger kinds cannot fly at all.

Make your own butterfly!

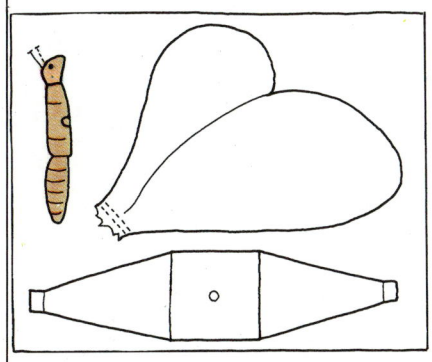

Cut out two wings like this from thin card and body, base and a square from thick card.

Glue the wings to the body, the square to the base and a pencil to the body so that it sticks downwards.

Glue the base to the wings. Push the pencil up and down through a hole in the base so the wings flap.

Shapes and controls of aircraft

Most aircraft today have the same basic shape of a long body with wings about halfway along on either side. At the back they have an upright fin and two horizontal ones which together are called the tailplane. The aircraft is controlled through control surfaces which are found on the rear edges of the wings, fin and tailplane. They are small panels which can be moved up and down to change the shape of the wing or fin. Those on the wings are called ailerons, those on the tailplane elevators.

If the elevators are lowered the top of the tailplane curves. This creates lift in the same way that a wing does. So the tail rises higher than the front of the aircraft and the plane dives. Movement to the left or right is controlled by the rudder on the rear fin of the plane.

△ Delta-winged aircraft have large, triangular-shaped wings and no tailplane. The British Vulcan bomber was the first large plane like this to be built. It dates from the 1950s. The bomber was controlled by 'elevons' which are control surfaces that all delta-winged aircraft have. Elevons combine the aileron and elevator controls that are used on ordinary planes. They are found on the rear edge of the wing.

◁ These are the elevons of a Concorde airliner. If both elevons move down, the plane dives. If one goes up and one down, the plane rolls sideways

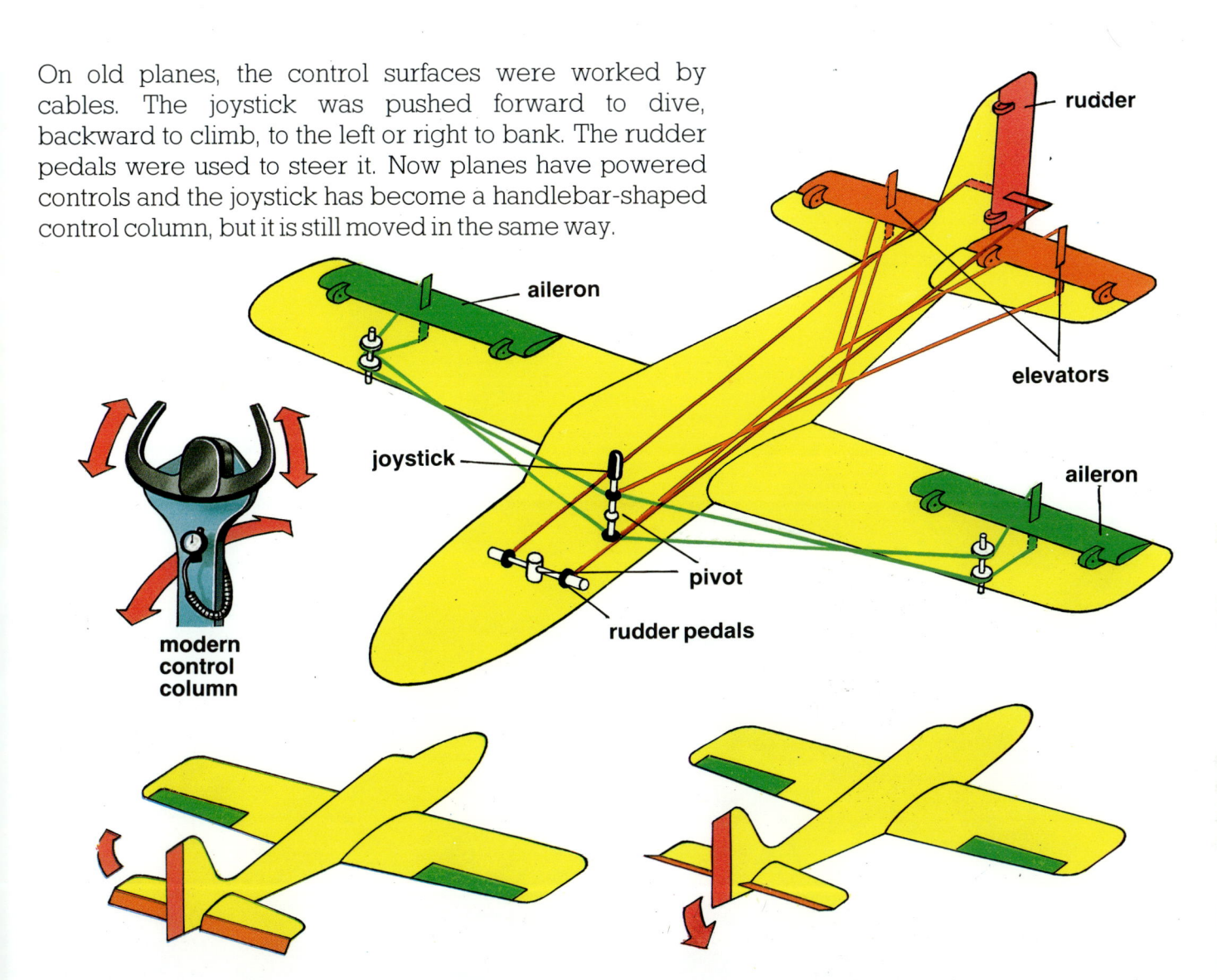

On old planes, the control surfaces were worked by cables. The joystick was pushed forward to dive, backward to climb, to the left or right to bank. The rudder pedals were used to steer it. Now planes have powered controls and the joystick has become a handlebar-shaped control column, but it is still moved in the same way.

Diving – the elevators go down, making the tailplane create more lift so that the tail rises. The nose drops and the plane dives until the elevators are moved the other way.

Climbing – the elevators go up to reduce the lift and make the tail drop. The nose rises and the plane climbs, providing there is enough engine power to pull it upwards.

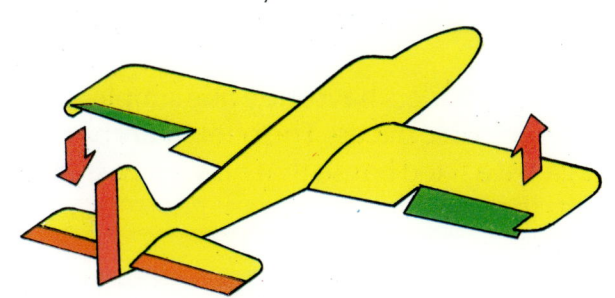

Banking left – the left aileron goes up, reducing the amount of lift created so the left wing drops. The right aileron goes down at the same time, increasing the lift so the right wing rises.

Turning left – the rudder is pushed to the left so that the tail swings to the right and the aircraft's nose swings to the left. The aircraft is also banked to the left when turning left.

Aircraft have been designed in many different shapes. In the early days of flying, biplanes were more usual than the single-winged planes we know today. They had two wings on either side, one above the other. There have been experimental planes with no body or tail at all. They were just like a large wing in the shape of a boomerang and the pilot and passengers sat inside it. Some supersonic planes which travel faster than the speed of sound do not have the

△ Hang gliders have only one simple wing with no control surfaces. The pilot steers by pushing against a fixed bar so that his weight shifts and tilts the glider.

two horizontal tailplane fins. Instead they have a triangular-shaped surface which sticks out from the body in front of the wings. Like the tailplane on other aircraft, this helps the plane fly on a smooth, level path.

Orbit and satellites

All objects are pulled towards each other by the force of gravity. The strength of the pull depends on their size. Since the Earth is larger than all the objects on it, the force of the Earth's gravity is so strong that it pulls all other objects to it. Gravity is not a force you can see, but it does affect everything on Earth. You cannot even escape it in space, the stars, planets and comets are all pulled together by gravity.

The orbiting Moon

When Newton (see page 6) saw the falling apple, he had been wondering why the Moon goes in a circle round the Earth. He saw that the Earth's gravity pulls the Moon towards the Earth in just the same way that it pulled the apple to the ground. The Moon moves sideways above the Earth. Without gravity, it would go off into space in a straight line and at a steady speed. There is no friction in space to slow it down. But the Earth's gravity pulls the Moon back, bending its path so that it goes round and round the Earth. This endless circle is called an orbit.

Any body in orbit is known as a satellite. The Earth and all the planets are satellites of the Sun. They are attracted to the Sun and orbit round it because of the pull of its gravity.

There are also stars which orbit each other, even though they may be the same size. Both go round – there is nothing in the middle of the circle.

▷ Communications satellites orbit far above the Earth. They are used to send television and telephone signals from one continent to another. Most communications satellites orbit in a path that keeps them above the same spot on the equator all the time. This type of orbit is called a synchronous orbit.

The satellites are built in specially clean rooms like the one shown here. A speck of dust could ruin them. The large dish-shaped objects at the top of the satellite are antennas used to pick up and send out the signals. Power for the satellite comes from solar panels which absorb energy from the Sun.

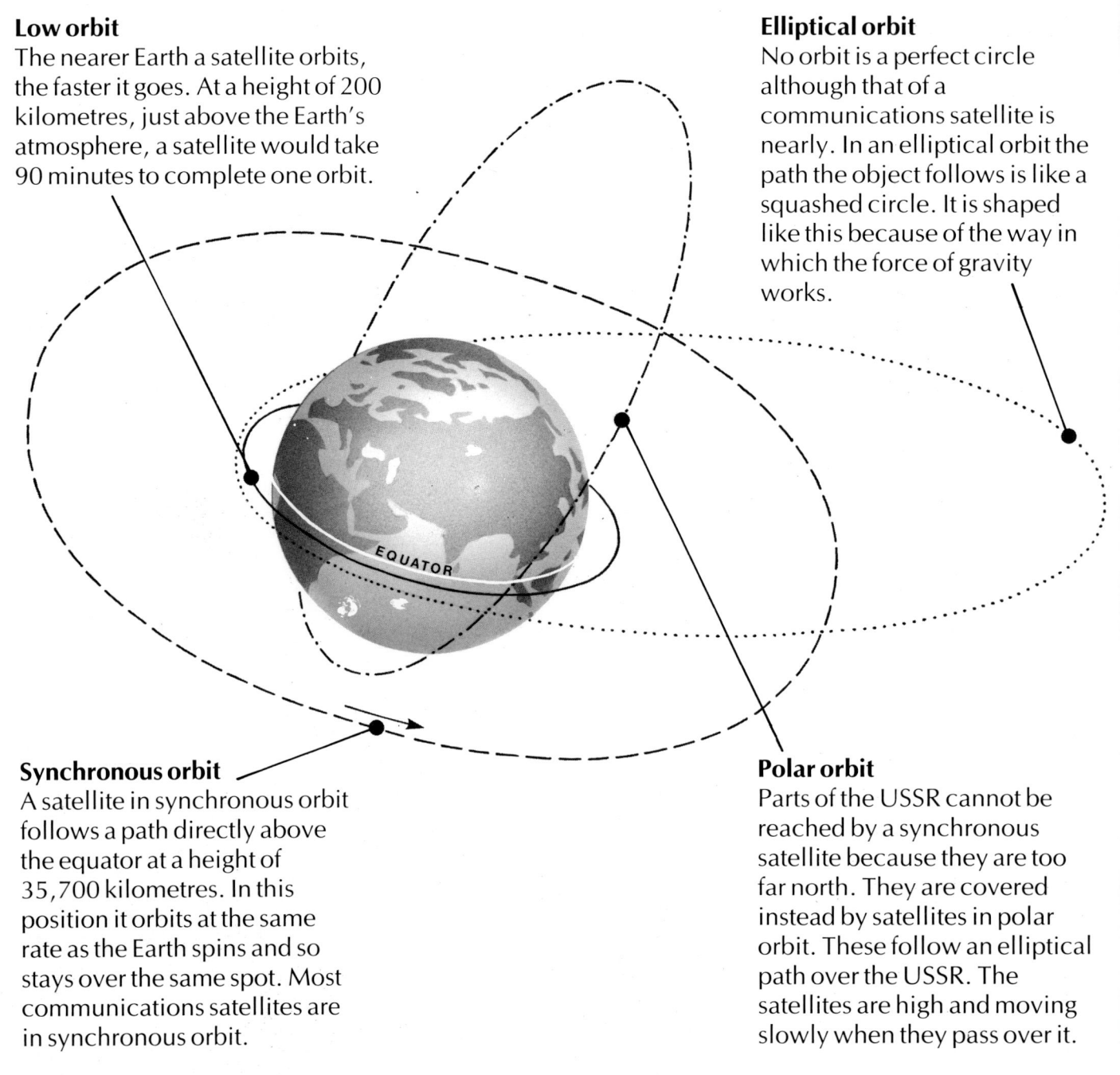

Low orbit
The nearer Earth a satellite orbits, the faster it goes. At a height of 200 kilometres, just above the Earth's atmosphere, a satellite would take 90 minutes to complete one orbit.

Elliptical orbit
No orbit is a perfect circle although that of a communications satellite is nearly. In an elliptical orbit the path the object follows is like a squashed circle. It is shaped like this because of the way in which the force of gravity works.

Synchronous orbit
A satellite in synchronous orbit follows a path directly above the equator at a height of 35,700 kilometres. In this position it orbits at the same rate as the Earth spins and so stays over the same spot. Most communications satellites are in synchronous orbit.

Polar orbit
Parts of the USSR cannot be reached by a synchronous satellite because they are too far north. They are covered instead by satellites in polar orbit. These follow an elliptical path over the USSR. The satellites are high and moving slowly when they pass over it.

If the Earth's gravity and the Moon's sideways movement balanced each other exactly, the Moon would move round the Earth in a perfect circle. But it does not. Instead it follows an elliptical orbit. This happens because of the pull of the Earth's gravity.

Gravity makes the Moon fall to the Earth as it goes around. As it nears the Earth, it speeds up because of the stronger pull of gravity. But the speeding up means that the sideways movement becomes stronger than the downward pull, so the Moon heads away again. As it gets farther from the Earth, gravity slows it again and it begins to fall back, so completing the orbit.

The orbit the Moon follows is shaped like a slightly squashed circle. Comets travel in a much more elliptical orbit, like a very squashed circle. They come near the Sun for a short time and then sweep off into space. Some stay out of sight for thousands of years.

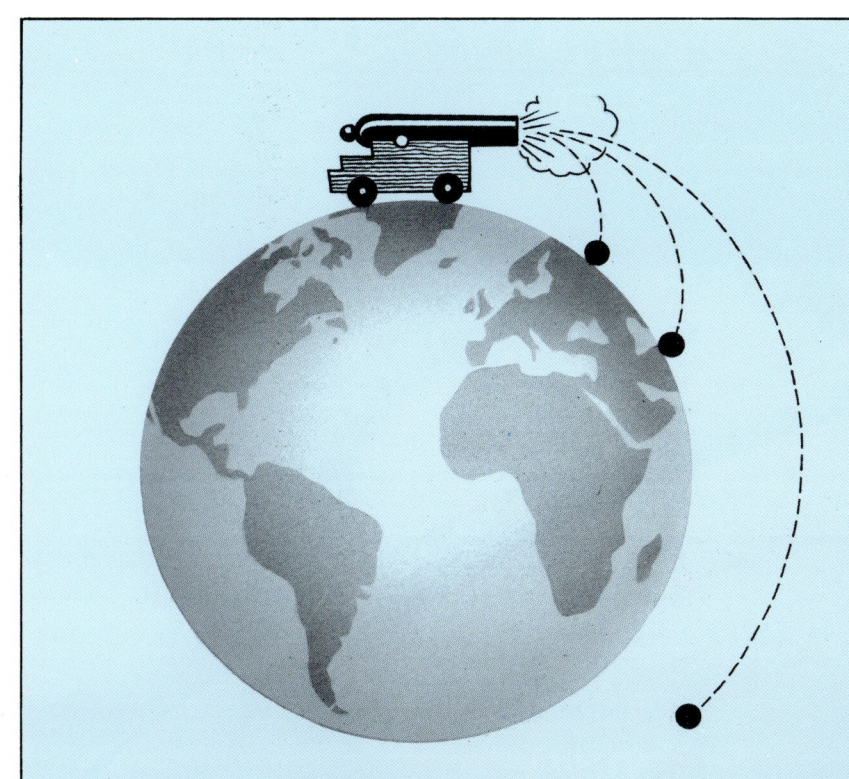

△ To understand orbit, think of a cannon. If it fires a ball slowly, gravity pulls the ball's path down and it soon falls to Earth. Fired faster, the ball falls further away. Fired very fast indeed, the ball's curved path stays so high that it never hits the Earth at all. Instead it goes right round it, into orbit. Satellites orbit above the Earth's atmosphere so there is no friction to slow them down.

▽ A comet is a mass of ice and dust which travels around the Sun in a huge elliptical orbit. When it gets near the Sun, radiation pouring out of the Sun tears away the outside of the comet, sending it streaming off in a bright 'tail'. Many comets have been seen but Halley's comet which is shown below is the brightest. It returns to the Sun every 76 years and is due to travel past Earth in 1986. Scientists will examine it closely then to try to find out more about exactly what comets are made of.